NATIONAL
ACADEMIES

Sciences
Engineering
Medicine

Essential Health Care Services Related to Anxiety and Mood Disorders in Women

Alexandra Andrada,
Melissa Maitin-Shepard,
Marian Flaxman, and
Sharyl J. Nass, *Rapporteurs*

Forum on Mental Health and
Substance Use Disorders

Board on Health Care Services

Health and Medicine Division

Proceedings of a Workshop

NATIONAL ACADEMIES PRESS 500 Fifth Street, NW Washington, DC 20001

This activity was supported by a contract between the National Academy of Sciences and the Health Resources and Services Administration (contract no. 75R60221D00002, purchase order no. 75FCMC22P0038). Any opinions, findings, conclusions, or recommendations expressed in this publication do not necessarily reflect the views of any organization or agency that provided support for the project.

International Standard Book Number-13: 978–0-309-72457-9
International Standard Book Number-10: 0–309-72457-0
Digital Object Identifier: https://doi.org/10.17226/27912

This publication is available from the National Academies Press, 500 Fifth Street, NW, Keck 360, Washington, DC 20001; (800) 624-6242 or (202) 334-3313; http://www.nap.edu.

Suggested citation: National Academies of Sciences, Engineering, and Medicine. 2024. *Essential health care services related to anxiety and mood disorders in women: Proceedings of a workshop.* Washington, DC: The National Academies Press. https://doi.org/10.17226/27912.

WORKSHOP PLANNING COMMITTEE

COLLEEN GALAMBOS (*Co-chair*), Helen Bader Endowed Chair in Applied Gerontology and Professor, Helen Bader School of Social Welfare, University of Wisconsin—Milwaukee

VIVIAN W. PINN (*Co-chair*), Former Director, Office of Research on Women's Health, National Institutes of Health (Retired); Former Senior Scientist Emerita, Fogarty International Center, National Institutes of Health

JAMILLE FIELDS ALLSBROOK, Assistant Professor, School of Law, Center for Health Law Studies, Saint Louis University

JOY BURKHARD, Founder and Executive Director, Policy Center for Maternal Mental Health

JILL M. EMANUELE, Vice President, Clinical Training, Child Mind Institute; Board Member and Secretary, Anxiety and Depression Association of America

TAMARA LEWIS JOHNSON, Program Director, Women's Mental Health Research Program, Office of Disparities Research and Workforce Diversity

JENNIFER LEONARDO, Director, Children's Safety Network, Education Development Center

HEIDI NELSON, Professor, Health Systems Science, Kaiser Permanente Bernard J. Tyson School of Medicine

J. NWANDO OLAYIWOLA, Chief Health Equity Officer and Senior Vice President, Humana, Inc.

GEORGE M. SLAVICH, Professor of Psychiatry and Biobehavioral Sciences; Director, Laboratory for Stress Assessment and Research; Investigator, Staglin One Mind Center for Cognitive Neuroscience; Research Scientist, Semel Institute for Neuroscience and Human Behavior, University of California, Los Angeles

Staff

ALEXANDRA ANDRADA, Forum Director/Program Officer
VIOLET BISHOP, Research Assistant
ANESIA WILKS, Senior Program Assistant
SHARYL J. NASS, Senior Director, Board on Health Care Services

Consultants

MELISSA MAITIN-SHEPARD, MMS Health Strategies, LLC
MARIAN FLAXMAN, Informed Solutions, LLC

Reviewers

This Proceedings of Essential Health Care Services Related to Anxiety and Mood Disorders in Women was reviewed in draft form by individuals chosen for their diverse perspectives and technical expertise. The purpose of this independent review is to provide candid and critical comments that will assist the National Academies of Sciences, Engineering, and Medicine in making each published proceedings as sound as possible and to ensure that it meets the institutional standards for quality, objectivity, evidence, and responsiveness to the charge. The review comments and draft manuscript remain confidential to protect the integrity of the process.

We thank the following individuals for their review of this proceedings:

KRYSTAL M. LEWIS, National Institute of Mental Health
MARY-FRANCES O'CONNER, University of Arizona

Although the reviewers listed above provided many constructive comments and suggestions, they were not asked to endorse the content of the proceedings nor did they see the final draft before its release. The review of this proceedings was overseen by **BRUCE CALONGE,** University of Colorado School of Medicine. He was responsible for making certain that an independent examination of this proceedings was carried out in accordance with standards of the National Academies and that all review comments were carefully considered. Responsibility for the final content rests entirely with the rapporteurs and the National Academies.

Acknowledgments

The National Academies of Sciences, Engineering, and Medicine are grateful for the support of the Health Resources Services Administration, which sponsored this workshop. The Forum on Mental Health and Substance Use Disorders wish to thank the planning committee cochairs Vivian W. Pinn and Colleen Galambos for their valuable contributions to the field of women's health and the development and organization of this workshop, in addition to the members of the planning committee, who collaborated to ensure a workshop complete with informative presentations and rich discussions.

The forum wishes to thank all the speakers who shared personal anecdotes and a lived experience perspective during the event: Schroeder Stribling, Ebony Carter, Tory Eisenlohr-Moul, Carla Perissinotto, Joy Burkhard, Alex Sheldon, Kimberly Aguillard, and Nicolle L. Arthun. Finally, the forum wants to thank all the speakers and moderators, who generously shared their expertise and their time with workshop attendees.

Support from the many sponsors of the Forum on Mental Health and Substance Use Disorders is critical to its work. The sponsors include the American College of Clinical Pharmacy, American Psychiatric Nurses Association, American Psychological Association, Centers for Disease Control and Prevention, Centers for Medicare & Medicaid Services, Council on Social Work Education, National Association of Addiction Treatment Providers, National Institutes of Health (National Institute on Alcohol Abuse and Alcoholism, National Institute on Drug Abuse, National Institute of Mental Health), Office of the Assistant Secretary for Planning and Evaluation, and Substance Abuse and Mental Health Services Administration.

Contents

Figures

FIGURES

Acronyms and Abbreviations

ACE	adverse childhood experience
ADHD	attention deficit hyperactivity disorder
AI/AN	American Indian and Alaska Native
CBT	cognitive behavioral therapy
CDC	Centers for Disease Control and Prevention
CMS	Centers for Medicare and Medicaid Services
CVD	cardiovascular disease
DBT	dialectical behavioral therapy
DSM-5	*Diagnostic and Statistical Manual of Mental Health Disorders, Fifth Edition*
EHR	electronic health record
FDA	U.S. Food and Drug Administration
HC	hormonal contraceptive
HRSA	Health Resources and Services Administration
IHS	Indian Health Service
IPT	interpersonal therapy
IPV	intimate partner violence

LGBTQ+   lesbian, gay, bisexual, transgender, queer, intersex, or asexual

MA   meta-analysis
MDD   major depressive disorder
MHA   Mental Health America
MIND   Mediterranean Intervention for Neurodegenerative Delay diet

NA   nucleus accumbens
NIH   National Institutes of Health
NIMH   National Institute of Mental Health

PGD   prolonged grief disorder
PMAD   perinatal mood and anxiety disorder
PMDD   premenstrual depressive disorder
PME   premenstrual exacerbation
PMS   premenstrual syndrome
PSWQ   Penn State Worry Questionnaire
PTSD   posttraumatic stress disorder

RCT   randomized controlled trial

SAMHSA   Substance Abuse and Mental Health Services Administration
SDOH   social determinants of health
SNRI   serotonin norepinephrine reuptake inhibitor
SSRI   selective serotonin reuptake inhibitor
SUD   substance use disorder
SWAN   Study of Women's Health Across the Nation

UCLA   University of California, Los Angeles
UCSF   University of California, San Francisco
UPSM   University of Pittsburgh School of Medicine

VMS   vasomotor symptoms

Proceedings of a Workshop

INTRODUCTION

Research suggests that women experience more anxiety and mood disorders than men, and social determinants of health (SDOH)—such as economic security, job opportunities, racism and discrimination, and violence—have a unique impact on women (Albert, 2015; Altemus et al., 2014; Bahrami and Yousefi, 2011). Additionally, the female life-span includes episodes of hormonal fluctuations—such as puberty, pregnancy, and menopause—that affect anxiety and mood differently. Despite these disparities, women's unique behavioral health[1] needs and strengths are accounted for inconsistently by health care providers and organizations and other components of the health care system (Chin et al., 2014). To address these challenges, and at the request of the Health Resources and Services Administration (HRSA),[2] the Forum on Mental Health and Substance Use Disorders at the National Academies of Sciences, Engineering, and Medicine (the National Academies) held a public workshop on April 29–30, 2024, to consider essential health care services related to anxiety and mood disorders in women. Colleen Galambos, Helen Bader Chair in Applied Gerontology and professor at the University of Wisconsin–Milwaukee, empha-

---

[1] SAMHSA defines behavioral health as the promotion of mental health, resilience, and well-being; the treatment of mental and substance use disorders; and the support of those who experience and/or are in recovery from these conditions, along with their families and communities. https://www.samhsa.gov/sites/default/files/samhsa-behavioral-health-integration.pdf (accessed June 6, 2024).

[2] See https://www.hrsa.gov/ (accessed June 10, 2024).

1

sized that the workshop was planned to explore essential health care services across the life-span for women experiencing anxiety and mood disorders and ways to improve outcomes for these populations. The content of the workshop will inform ongoing HRSA behavioral health efforts to improve short- and long-term health outcomes for women.

The workshop included seven sessions and featured subject-matter experts who shared presentations on anxiety and mood disorders across the female life-span. Such topics included the importance of screening for postpartum depression; the power of community care for improving health outcomes and reducing health disparities; the importance of prevention in addition to recognizing, diagnosing, and treating anxiety and mood disorders in children and adolescents; the impact of hormones in elevating risk for anxiety and mood disorders and hormone therapies for treatment; midlife and menopause and how both hormonal and nonhormonal therapies may be beneficial for treating anxiety and mood disorders during this period; healthy approaches to aging and unique social factors that affect older adults; the policy landscape for women's mental health care; lessons that can be learned from special populations and how those lessons might be applied to policy or the provision of clinical care; and potential ways to improve the provision of care and future directions for women's mental health services. The appendixes consist of the statement of task, the workshop agenda, and the readings and resources provided to attendees. All meeting materials and recording of the workshop have been archived online.[3] This Proceedings of a Workshop[4] summarizes these presentations and discussions.

OVERVIEW OF WOMEN'S MENTAL HEALTH IN THE UNITED STATES

Schroeder Stribling, president and CEO of Mental Health America (MHA), said that women in the United States are more isolated and disconnected than ever, referring to the lingering impact of the COVID-19 pandemic. She highlighted MHA's National Prevention and Screening

---

Program,[5] which is accessed online by approximately 15,000 people each day. Two out of three people who use it identify as female and are under the age of 24, reflecting the mental distress of a younger generation. According to 2023 MHA data, 80 percent of people who took the screening and identified as female scored higher for being at risk of a mental health condition. In addition, 30 percent identified as survivors of trauma, 60 percent experienced anxiety related to body image or self-image, and 35 percent had suicidal ideation. Overall, the prevalence of these characteristics was higher among women. People who identified as Black, multiracial, or lesbian, gay, bisexual, transgender, queer, intersex, or asexual (LGBTQ+) had particularly high rates of mental health risk factors compared to female participants overall.

Stribling said that this disproportionate burden of mental health conditions among women has generally been viewed through a sociocultural lens; compared to men, women do more emotional labor, are subject to bias and discrimination, are more vulnerable to violence, and are more likely to be exploited than men. She added that COVID-19 has further eroded mental health, correlating with a decline in physical activity and a loss of financial stability and social connectedness. Stribling emphasized that the way mental health is addressed in society is maladaptive. She spoke of the benefits of a more holistic approach that fosters community; incorporates nature; elevates purpose, meaning, and belonging; and inspires connection to a greater purpose than oneself. Stribling noted that neuroscience research shows that spiritual connection has a benefit for cognitive health, is protective against risk for mental illness, and supports recovery. "We in the healing profession," Stribling said, "can lead the way in integrating these concepts into the paradigm of health." Furthermore, integrating holistic and complementary practices into primary care would increase access to mental health care services.

Stribling stressed the importance of addressing social inequities and suggested that mental health professionals collaborate with allies in both research and advocacy. She emphasized an opportunity for health care professionals to "lead not only with science and rigor, but also with authenticity and with heart" and reminded them about the importance of taking care of their own health to allow them to continue to perform their work effectively.

Stribling said that she sees opportunities to define the future of whole-person health and healing to promote human flourishing. She described the benefits of caring for the whole person, including mind, body, and spirit, adding that integrative, holistic, and complementary practices could be integrated into primary care to make them more affordable and accessible. Stribling challenged the limitations of the medical model and suggested that the future of health emphasize and encourage prevention rather than focus on pathology.

---

[5] See https://screening.mhanational.org/screening-tools/ (accessed June 11, 2024).

In closing, Stribling elevated the voice of one of MHA's young national leaders: "mental health is not about mental health care; it's about purpose and meaning and finding the things that make life worth living." She noted her optimism about the future of the field of women's mental health care, stating that the efforts of workshop participants would create a brighter future for all.

THE PERINATAL PERIOD

The first session focused on women experiencing anxiety and mood disorders during the perinatal period—defined as from conception to up to a year after birth. It included an introduction by moderator and planning committee member Tamara Lewis Johnson, program director for Women's Mental Health Research in the Office of Disparities Research and Workforce Diversity at the National Institute of Mental Health (NIMH), and featured presentations from Crystal Clark, assistant professor in the Department of Psychiatry at the University of Toronto and associate head of research at the Women's College Hospital; Catherine Monk, Inaugural Diana Vagelos Professor of Women's Health in the Department of Obstetrics & Gynecology at Columbia University Vagelos College of Physicians and Surgeons and research scientist at New York State Psychiatric Institute; and Ebony Carter, division director of maternal and fetal medicine at the University of North Carolina School of Medicine.

Lewis Johnson stated that mental health disorders, such as anxiety and depression, are widely understood to be the most common complications of pregnancy and childbirth; 15–21 percent of pregnant and postpartum women experience perinatal mood and anxiety disorders (PMADs) (Hernandez et al., 2022). She also highlighted racial disparities, noting that Black women are more likely to experience PMADs compared with White women. Specifically, younger Black women on public insurance are more likely to have PMADs, and more than 40 percent of Black women experience postpartum depression—more than double the rate of the general population. Black women, she said, are also less likely to receive a follow-up appointment to address mental health diagnoses. Lewis Johnson also stated that untreated maternal mental health disorders increase the risk of suicidal behaviors, noting that 8 percent of perinatal populations worldwide experience suicidal ideation, which has increased 100 percent between 2008 and 2018 (Kobylski et al., 2023).

PMADs: Understanding Risk and Moving Toward Solutions

Clark spoke about the prevalence, risks, and treatments of PMADs. She began by explaining that these disorders, including anxiety, depression, and bipolar disorder, exist on a spectrum. Anxiety disorders include social anxiety, obsessive compulsive disorder, phobias, panic disorder, and generalized anxiety disorder. Another common mental health disorder is posttraumatic stress disorder (PTSD). It impacts five of every 100 U.S. adults (VA, n.d.). It develops as the result of a trauma and can be debilitating. Although PTSD was considered a type of anxiety disorder, Clark noted that it is now classified in the *Diagnostic and Statistical Manual of Mental Disorders, Fifth Edition* (DSM-5) as a trauma- and stressor-related disorder. Clark pointed to sex differences in diagnosis of anxiety and mood disorders; women are twice as likely as men to be diagnosed with anxiety and have PTSD. Clark said that PTSD can occur as a result of experiences such as sexual or birth trauma. She noted that data indicate that 10 percent of childbearing people will have PTSD during their lifetime (Cook et al., 2018). However, Clark said, rates of bipolar disorder are about equal between men and women (Wisner et al., 2013).

One in five childbearing people have a mood or anxiety disorder during the perinatal period. Although postpartum depression is most commonly discussed, Clark noted that much of this depression actually begins during pregnancy, and up to 27 percent begins preconception. The data on prevalence of perinatal depression and anxiety are thought to be underestimates, as it is estimated that up to 20 percent of people are not identified by screening (WHO, 2022). With this context in mind, Clark said that the data suggest that 33 percent of pregnant people will experience the onset of depressive symptoms, and 40 percent will have postpartum depression.

Bipolar disorder, Clark said, is understudied and represents an important area of future research. Estimates suggest that 20 percent of potential diagnoses are missed during screenings (Wisner et al., 2013), and these individuals thus lack access to treatment and services. Among people with a pre-existing bipolar diagnosis, 71 percent have a recurrence during the perinatal period, Clark said (Viguera et al., 2007). That can be due to a variety of factors, particularly discontinuing prescribed bipolar medication during pregnancy or breastfeeding (Viguera et al., 2000, 2007).

Perinatal mental illness, Clark said, is associated with intrauterine growth retardation, preterm birth, low birthweight, and preeclampsia (Howard and Khalifeh, 2020). Maternal behaviors associated with mental illness also may have negative impacts on the fetus and previous children. Mothers struggling with mental illness may be more likely to self-medicate, misuse substances, skip prenatal care, or engage in other risky behaviors. Additionally, Clark noted, maternal mental illness can have specific negative impacts on both the mother and child during the postpartum period. Women may wish to avoid psychiatric medication during breastfeeding, for example, or do not have time for psychotherapy. Clark said that in addition to negatively impacting the mother, this lack of mental health care has measurable effects on child development. She said that children raised by mothers with clinical depression perform lower on tests of cognitive ability (Center on the Developing Child, 2009) and measures of emotional and behavioral performance.

Another diagnosis impacting women in the perinatal period is postpartum psychosis, which usually occurs within the first 4 weeks postpartum and affects one in 1,000 women (Bergink et al., 2016). Postpartum women with a history of bipolar diagnosis have a 50 percent higher risk of postpartum psychosis. It often includes cognitive symptoms, such as disorganized thoughts and lack of insight and judgment. It is a psychiatric emergency, Clark said, as it is the leading cause of maternal suicide and infanticide.

Clark detailed the racial and ethnic disparities in perinatal mental health, with a particular focus on Black maternal mental health (Haight et al., 2024). Clark said that both Black and Asian women are less likely to receive a mental illness diagnosis or receive follow-up care compared with White women. She noted the many confounders in this research, but rates of mental health disorders are consistently found to be higher among U.S. people of color compared to their White counterparts. Clark highlighted the critical topic of Black maternal mortality, which is elevated in the United States. Black birthing people have mortality rates that are 2.6 times higher than their White counterparts, and nearly a quarter of these deaths are attributable to postpartum suicide;[6] the risk is highest during the 9–12 month postpartum period, Clark said.

There are also racial disparities in infant health outcomes. Clark stated that Black infants face a 2.3 times higher rate of infant mortality and are twice as likely to be considered "low birthweight" when compared with White infants. Clark added that although all birthing people are at risk for postpartum depression, complications such as preterm birth, low socioeconomic status, and a history of trauma, and lack of postpartum social support increase the risk (Robertson et al., 2004). Clark added that women with health conditions impacted by SDOH are at higher risk for excess maternal and infant mortality. She also stated that Hispanic women also have elevated risk and are also often undiagnosed or untreated for existing mental health disorders. Furthermore, research is minimal on those who identify as LGBTQ+, she added.

Clark said that screening for mental health disorders in the perinatal period is essential (Admon et al., 2021; Sidebottom et al., 2021; Tabb et al., 2023). She noted that it may be ineffective because the screenings are often not culturally sensitive. She asserted that PMADs are treatable and discussed available options, including psychotherapy and pharmacotherapy. She said that pharmacotherapy is the mainstay for bipolar disorder and for moderate to severe mood disorders. Clark noted that the U.S. Food and Drug Administration (FDA) recently approved two medications, brexanolone and zuranolone,

---

[6] See https://www.cdc.gov/media/releases/2022/p0919-pregnancy-related-deaths.html (accessed June 11, 2024).

specifically for postpartum depression, but their high costs put them out of reach for most women (Deligiannidis et al., 2021). Clark also mentioned social support interventions (Almanza et al., 2022), including doulas, midwives, birth centers, lactation counselors, and telehealth services. She also described "psycho-hairapy," a community approach in which women participate in conversations about their mental health in a setting that is comfortable and familiar, such as the hair salon. These types of services, Clark noted, have shown promise, especially in Black communities. In closing, Clark said that her goal is to enable a world in which all perinatal women, birthing people, and parents can survive and thrive.

Prevention, Treatment, and Impact of PMADs

Monk emphasized that PMADs are real, measurable, treatable, and preventable. She reiterated that women are at a greater lifetime risk for mental health disorders compared with men. This disparity may be attributed to their additional psychosocial stressors, such as income inequality, additional caregiving responsibilities, greater levels of emotional stress, the need to balance paid and unpaid labor, higher rates of discrimination in the workplace, higher rates of childhood abuse and neglect, and the impact of intimate partner violence (IPV), said Monk (Platt et al., 2016). Additionally, women experience the unique biological impact of female sex hormones during puberty, pregnancy, and menopause.

Monk highlighted the role of SDOH in the excessive burden of mental health disorders in women, with a specific focus on location and access to services. She illustrated this geographic disparity by comparing access to social services in California and Alabama.[7] California has an expanded Medicaid system, supports in the postpartum period, and additional government-funded support for families. In contrast, Alabama has not expanded Medicaid to the same extent, and government-funded social support is much less. The national average rate of postpartum mental health conditions is 21.9 percent; by comparison, it is 17.1 percent in California but 27.6 percent in Alabama (Zero to Three, 2022). Monk argued that this illustrates the role that basic access to social services plays in preventing postpartum mental health disorders.

Monk described a report from the Substance Abuse and Mental Health Services Administration (SAMHSA) that highlighted the levels of trauma that can impact mental health (SAMHSA, 2023). In addition to individual trauma, Monk noted the roles of family, group, community, collective, historical, racial, and mass trauma (see Figure 1).

---

[7] See https://stateofbabies.org/ (accessed June 12, 2024).

8

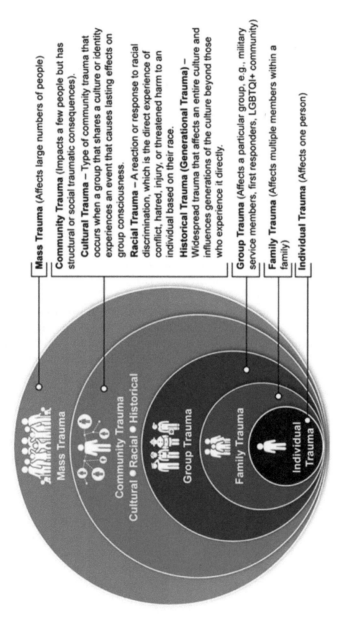

Mass Trauma (Affects large numbers of people)

Community Trauma (Impacts a few people but has structural or social traumatic consequences).

Cultural Trauma – Type of community trauma that occurs when a group that shares a culture or identity experiences an event that causes lasting effects on group consciousness.

Racial Trauma – A reaction or response to racial discrimination, which is the direct experience of conflict, hatred, injury, or threatened harm to an individual based on their race.

Historical Trauma (Generational Trauma) – Widespread trauma that affects an entire culture and influences generations of the culture beyond those who experience it directly.

Group Trauma (Affects a particular group, e.g., military service members, first responders, LGBTQI+ community)

Family Trauma (Affects multiple members within a family)

Individual Trauma (Affects one person)

FIGURE 1 Levels of trauma experience.

SOURCES: Presented by Catherine Monk on April 29, 2024; SAMHSA, 2023. This material is used courtesy of the Substance Abuse and Mental Health Services Administration: Practical Guide for Implementing a Trauma-Informed Approach. HHS Publication No. PEP23-06-05-005 Rockville, MD: National Mental Health and Substance Abuse Use Policy Laboratory. Substance Abuse and Mental Health Services Administration, 2023.

Next, Monk spoke about the biology of PMADs. She illustrated the changes that occur in the brain during the transition to motherhood by depicting brain scans and charts that compared measurements of cortical thickness during a pregnancy versus other periods in the life-span (Carmona et al., 2019). Monk noted the changes in the reduction in gray matter during pregnancy and linked them to the dramatic changes within the brain over the course of adolescence. She highlighted that these reductions specifically occur in areas of the brain associated with emotional regulation and mood, including the prefrontal cortex and hippocampus, and that this remodeling may enable alterations in circuits that support the different emotional demands and identity shifts that come with becoming a parent (Servin-Barthet et al., 2023).

Monk said the perinatal period is a time of significant brain changes, which are primed and driven by dramatic changes in hormones such as estrogen, progesterone, cortisol, and oxytocin. She also noted that postpartum breastfeeding causes changes in hormones that can have a similar effect.

Monk reiterated that PMADs are not merely a social phenomenon but biologically rooted illnesses involving complex interactions among stress, trauma, hormones, and the brain. Monk added that women with a history of trauma may be especially sensitive to these changes and more likely to have their hypothalamic-pituitary-adrenal axis destabilized by hormonal shifts, driving destabilizing changes to their mood (Di Benedetto et al., 2024). When social stressors, such as housing or food insecurity, are added, Monk said, they can cause a dramatic cascade.

Monk explained that research from her lab has examined differences in the newborn brain between babies born to mothers with and without depression and anxiety. She noted observable differences in brain connectivity, with less connectivity between the prefrontal cortex and amygdala in babies born to mothers with depression. This suggests a brain that is primed for reactivity, as this early stage may have less connectivity enabling the prefrontal cortex to dampen amygdala responses to stimuli, potentially contributing to leaving them vulnerable to mental health conditions, Monk explained. Other research has shown that babies born to mothers with anxiety show greater neuronal response to aberrant sound (Sylvester et al., 2021) in areas associated with anxiety disorders in adults.

Monk echoed the concern of undiagnosed physical and mental health conditions. A lack of diagnosis can prevent treatment and contribute to worsening health outcomes in women, children, and families. Monk cited a 2019 study that followed women without any diagnosed mental health conditions (Walsh et al., 2019) and illustrated the importance of moving beyond a basic understanding of health and examining the role of stress and SDOH in overall health outcomes of women and babies. Monk also cited a 2022 study from her group examining women with bipolar disorder during pregnancy (Babineau et al., 2022). They were all receiving comprehensive psychiatric care, but some were "non-responders" with high symptoms of anxiety and depression, despite pharmacological treatment. The non-responders had higher levels of childhood trauma: 87 percent compared with 50 percent in the responder group. Monk stated that women with a history of childhood trauma who do not respond to pharmacological treatment may require a multipronged approach, including psychotherapy, at minimum.

Monk noted that the largest impediment to recovering from PMADs is a lack of access to treatment and reiterated the importance of community and social support. She listed some programs that provide social support, education, and awareness to prevent and treat PMADs: Reach Out Stay Strong Essentials, Mothers and Babies, and Practical Resources for Effective Postpartum Parenting. Columbia University offers virtual support groups for pregnant and postpartum people and their partners and babies. For example, "Birth of a Parent, Birth of a Child" allows new mothers to have their questions answered and find community. Furthermore, helping women learn to anticipate hormonal surges attributed to mood changes can help make symptoms easier to manage, Monk noted. These types of programs are feasible and scalable, and she encouraged clinical care professionals to look to community experts for tools that can be integrated into the clinical care setting.

Elevating Reproductive Health Equity

Ebony Carter introduced EleVATE (Elevating Voices, Addressing Depression, Toxic Stress, and Equity in Group Prenatal Care Women's Collaborative), which is a community-based program that launched in 2016. During this time, preterm birth rates in the city of St. Louis were high, E. Carter said. A "meeting of the minds" was called to address the poor postpartum health outcomes, which initiated an agreement between maternal and infant health care providers working in practices and health systems across the city, transdisciplinary care providers, patients, and community members to work together to improve maternal and infant health outcomes in St. Louis, forming EleVATE.

E. Carter described group prenatal care as "not the typical 10-minute visit." It allows for more time for answering questions, education and support, discussion of topics such as postpartum depression, and baby care techniques, she said. It involves women around the same gestational age, meeting together in groups of 6–10, every 2–4 weeks, for approximately 90–120 minutes per session. E. Carter cited a study that found patients who were randomized into a group prenatal care model saw a 33 percent reduction in risk for preterm birth, compared with those receiving usual prenatal care. In a subgroup of Black patients, the reduction was so great (41 percent) that it eliminated the racial disparity in preterm birth rates in the city (Ickovics et al., 2007); this was the first intervention that had ever been shown to do so. E. Carter's research group published a meta-analysis that found that group care did not reduce preterm birth rate overall, but for a Black subgroup, it did so by 45 percent (Carter et al., 2016).

E. Carter shared a map of St. Louis that illustrated geographic, racial, and socioeconomic disparities in preterm birth rates. She noted that the more affluent and White neighborhoods had lower preterm birth rates and better maternal health outcomes compared with lower-income, Black neighborhoods. EleVATE also works to address these health inequities. For context, she noted that the project formed not long after Michael Brown, a young Black man, was killed only 8 miles from where these maternal health practitioners were working. The community work done by the Ferguson Commission report,[8] in the wake of this tragic shooting, was impactful to the development of EleVATE, she said.

E. Carter shared the challenges experienced at the start of the project. The community voices, whom she referred to as "patients-turned-partners," had a deep-seated distrust of researchers and believed that research would lead to exploitation of the community. However, E. Carter, a researcher herself, argued that it was a necessary component and would enable the community to share their story with others. The participants ultimately agreed to a basic program evaluation, making sure that the program was held accountable to the voices of the community.

A major aim of the collaborative was to seek out the root causes of maternal mental health disparities, going beneath the level of SDOH. Issues addressed included power and wealth imbalances, class oppression, and gender discrimination. Community partners also identified mental health inequities. Despite screenings for mental health issues, Missouri Medicaid did not provide robust coverage of mental health services, leaving clinicians in a difficult position of not knowing where to refer a patient. E. Carter added that for some patients with both mental health issues and chronic illness, the combined burden of care felt impossible to manage.

E. Carter noted the importance of sharing information publicly so others could benefit and learn from their experiences. The program sought to achieve clinical improvements without critiquing the behaviors of patients. Patients are not the problem, E. Carter said. Instead, the program focused on clinician education and behaviors and improvements to the health care system as a whole. She specified that their program planning continually considered who would benefit from specific recommendations, including the potential for differential impacts among racial and ethnic groups. She noted that the organizers sought to bring in new ideas and make the group fully representa-

---

[8] See https://forwardthroughferguson.org/ (accessed June 12, 2024).

tive of the patient population. The project involved multiple teams charged with creating an effective prenatal care intervention, including a curriculum team that created a care plan with evidence-based behavioral health techniques embedded in all group activities. The concept was to turn an obstetrical clinic into a mental health "extender," which included a robust referral network for issues that could not be addressed through the group program. The evaluation team was the research arm, responsible for evaluating the effectiveness of each intervention. The steering committee, composed of clinicians, patients, and other interested groups, set the overall tone for the program and continues to meet every 3 months.

E. Carter described the trainings that are required of all participating clinicians and staff. Staff at all levels have mandatory annual trainings on cultural competency and trauma-informed care practices, which empowers them to provide compassion and care. Staff are also required to complete 8 hours of Crossroads Anti-Racism[9] training and 16 hours of group care facilitation and behavioral health training. She noted that "patients-turned-partners" administer the trainings, which has been empowering for everyone involved. People have the opportunity to turn their own lived experiences into trainings that empower clinicians to practice more informed care.

E. Carter pointed to challenges that her team experienced while creating and implementing EleVATE, such as obtaining grants, due to the mismatch between community needs and the requirements of traditional grant applications. The patient voice and patient trust were always prioritized, which maintained the ethics and integrity of the program, even during times of financial hardship. She reiterated the importance of having a trusted voice in the community who can function as a translator and trusted broker. They maintain contact with the community, transcend the health care relationship, and represent the community voice with other partners. E. Carter said for EleVATE, this person was their program manager, who maintained a positive relationship with the community through activities such as sending birthday cards and attending community social events.

E. Carter discussed the pilot study findings from the initial intervention group (Lenze et al., 2024). The study was a proof of concept, she said, and had a small sample size ($n = 48$) that was not powered to show major differences. However, she also said that no patient in the group care model had a preterm birth, which was very different from the overall rate in the city (18 percent). Meaningful trends toward improvement in mental health outcomes were also observed but did not reach statistical significance.

E. Carter also provided an update on the status of the program, saying that it is supported by R01 grant funding from NIMH and funded at eight

---

[9] See https://crossroadsantiracism.org/ (accessed June 12, 2024).

sites across Missouri, covering 80 percent of Black patients in the state. Each site implements the program differently to understand how the different styles impact effectiveness. E. Carter also said she observed how the project increased physician empathy, and research is underway to further understand the impact of the program on clinicians. Obtaining funding for and conducting community-engaged work is difficult, she said, but her team remains committed to the process.

E. Carter quoted Reverend Starsky Wilson, cochair of the Ferguson Commission and CEO of the Children's Defense Fund: "Programs are short-term interventions that create temporary improvements in the wake of challenges. Policies, on the other hand, are covenants we collectively choose to live by, as articulated in legislation and regulation. They inform our socially accepted mores and ethics." E. Carter stated that the goal for EleVATE was not to merely create a program but to create lasting change through better health policies. This experience changed the direction of clinician–patient conversations and the care provided. In closing, E. Carter stated her belief that patients have "the most important voice at the table."

Discussion

Moderator Lewis Johnson asked Clark about access to perinatal psychiatric care, particularly in remote areas, which may have limited clinicians who provide this type of care. Clark replied that virtual resources are available and specifically suggested HRSA's National Maternal Health Hotline (Mom's Hotline),[10] which is available to anyone to receive expert advice and assistance. In addition, Postpartum Support International offers many free services, information, and guidance. E. Carter added the potential for using other types of care providers as mental health "extenders," suggesting that, within EleVATE, clinicians be trained and empowered to provide mental health resources and support.

Tory Eisenlohr-Moul, associate professor of psychiatry and psychology and associate director of translational research in women's mental health, University of Illinois–Chicago College of Medicine, asked the speakers about critical areas for future research, such as gender diversity. Clark replied that demographics such as race, ethnicity, sexual orientation, and gender identity are not historically well captured in this area of research. Gender identity has generally been captured by asking study participants for their pronouns, which may not yield the full picture of gender expressions or identity. She suggested that a starting place may be to improve the questions asked in research, with the goal of better capturing gender identity. Monk added that training on the

---

[10] See https://mchb.hrsa.gov/national-maternal-mental-health-hotline/faq# (accessed June 12, 2024).

topic, alongside improvements in the functionality of electronic health records (EHRs), can help to reduce patient stress in engaging with medical care providers about their identities. E. Carter added that recent research has found that 4 percent of the birthing people in her samples do not identify as women.

Jamille Fields Allsbrook, assistant professor in the School of Law at the Center for Health Law Studies, St. Louis University, asked E. Carter about her team's experience with "patients-turned-partners," noting that it can be difficult to develop and maintain these relationships. E. Carter responded that her team invited patients to have a prominent seat at the decision-making table from the beginning. She reiterated the importance of their voice and benefits of a community liaison to ensure that the community is seen, heard, and engaged. E. Carter explained that building trust takes time. Although she is a Black woman, the community viewed her as an academic first, so she had to work to earn their trust and fully commit herself to the process of building trust. She suggested that the National Institutes of Health (NIH) provide support for this process by tying funding to the process of community building. Dedicated time for trust and community building is not aligned with research demands or the incentive structures of academia, but incentives could be shifted by the grant-issuing bodies, Clark said.

Inger Burnett-Zeigler, associate professor of psychiatry and behavioral sciences at Northwestern University Feinberg School of Medicine, asked about the role of race, distinct from socioeconomic status, in informing maternal health outcomes. She noted that in the United States, Black women in higher-income brackets who have more education are still at risk for worse outcomes. She asked for suggestions to address this disparity. Clark suggested further research to explore the impact of racial factors and socioeconomic factors. Racism is an ongoing structural determinant of health, she said. She also recommended more community-based approaches to health care and stressed the benefits of greater representation of different racial groups in the health care setting. It takes time to train and grow the health care workforce, Clark noted, so it is even more important to empower different levels of community care support. Monk added that NIH could require grant-funded projects to include community members alongside principal investigators. She said that her work focuses on learnings from the restorative justice movement, including ways to acknowledge the roots of obstetrics' exploitation of Black women's bodies (Nnoli, 2023). Monk added that it is critical to acknowledge the impact of different types of stress on preterm birth rates and work with community partners to help patients address their basic needs, improve social networking, and mitigate stress. E. Carter added that, although race is a social construct, the effects of racism can be biological, and education status and wealth may not be protective against it. Until the root causes of systemic racism are addressed, E. Carter said, outcomes are unlikely to change.

Jennifer Leonardo, director of the Children's Safety Network at the Education Development Center and planning committee member, asked Monk about potential reasons for the gap between screening for symptoms and receiving care. Monk said that some clinicians do not know where to refer a patient after screening. Payment is also a major barrier, and Monk highlighted the potential for policy changes to enable access to mental health care, such as expanded coverage under Medicaid and improving the reimbursement rate so more providers will accept it. She noted that an incentive program could be created, offering student loan repayment to practitioners who provide mental health care to low-income populations just as for those who pursue clinical research. The session closed by reiterating the importance of diversifying the mental health care workforce and making such care more accessible for all.

CHILDHOOD AND ADOLESCENCE

The second featured a panel discussion moderated by planning committee member Jill M. Emanuele, vice president of clinical training and clinical psychologist at the Child Mind Institute. She introduced the speakers: Jennifer Leonardo; Mary Alvord, psychologist and director at Alvord, Baker, and Associates, LLC; and Krystal M. Lewis, clinical psychologist in the Section on Development and Affective Neurosciences at NIMH.

Emanuele highlighted the importance of primary prevention, screening, diagnosis, and treatment of anxiety and mood disorders in childhood and adolescence[11] and discussed statistics emphasizing the scope of the problem and their impact throughout a person's life. For example, she stated that experiencing major depressive episodes in childhood increases the likelihood of one in adulthood. Additionally, she said that an important focus of the conversation would be on strategies to increase coping skills for children and adolescents to enhance adaptability and reduce the symptoms and impact of mental health disorders and their adverse outcomes.

Lewis defined anxiety disorders as mental health conditions characterized by excessive fear, worry, or nervousness that is disproportionate to the situation. These disorders are also known to negatively impact daily life. Anxiety disorders are one of the most common forms of psychopathologies seen in children, Lewis said, with estimates suggesting that 9.4 percent of youth experience them (CDC, 2023), and have a lifetime prevalence rate of 32 percent for adolescents.[12] Untreated anxiety can lead to other mental health issues including mood disorders, contributing to the growing burden of mental health disorders in adulthood, Lewis said. Lewis noted that many such issues are rooted in

---

[11] Childhood is defined as birth to 12 years old, and adolescence includes ages 12–17.

[12] See https://adaa.org/understanding-anxiety/facts-statistics (accessed June 21, 2024).

childhood. Data show a gap of about 10 years between the onset of anxiety and depressive symptoms and when people seek mental health services (Wang et al., 2004). It is important to consider, Lewis said, what occurs during that period.

For anxiety disorders, Lewis discussed the data from the NIMH National Comorbidity Study, which showed that women and girls have a higher lifetime prevalence compared to men and boys; it also varied by age, race/ethnicity, and other sociocultural factors. For mood disorders, Emanuele said that 19.5 percent of children aged 12–17 had a major depressive episode between 2009 and 2019, and estimated prevalence is expected to have increased (SAMHSA, 2022). She also noted that diagnosing depression in children can be challenging because they do not always appear to be sad but instead may present as irritable or with psychosomatic complaints. Emanuele also discussed the challenges in managing mood dysregulation, especially in terms of proper diagnosis and effective treatment, as it is a transdiagnostic concern; these conditions do not always fit under a single criterion.

Emanuele asked Alvord to speak about effective prevention-focused interventions that support the mental health of children and adolescents. Alvord founded and operated a nonprofit, Resilience Across Borders,[13] aimed at providing mental health care to economically marginalized youth in the Washington, DC metro area. It trains teachers, classrooms, schools, and children to address and prevent mental health concerns. Alvord said that prevention is rooted in resilience. Using the imagery of a rubber band, Alvord described how it can be stretched to a certain point but may eventually snap if it is stretched too far or too many times. It is important to develop early coping skills, Alvord said, to improve mental flexibility and resilience and avoid "snapping" like the rubber band.

Alvord provided an acronym to highlight the important concepts related to child and adolescent mental health: ECAMPS. The E stands for "evidence based," and Alvord said that it is important to use evidence-based approaches. C stands for "cultural context," she said, and detailed her own experience growing up in a non-English-speaking household. She noted that language is merely one barrier and that there may also be cultural barriers to accessing care. C also stands for "coping," because research has shown that it is one of the most important skills for preventing mental health issues in children, Alvord said. M stands for "media," which plays an important role in disseminating mental health resources and information and also includes digital literacy. Alvord also noted that it can perpetuate misinformation about mental health. P stands for "problem solving" and being "proactive." The final letter was S, which she said stands for "skills." It is important to teach skills to youth, such as problem solving, to help them navigate mental health issues, Alvord said.

---

[13] See https://resilienceacrossborders.org/ (accessed June 20, 2024).

Emanuele asked Lewis what evidenced-based treatments are most effective for anxiety and mood disorders in youth. Lewis first noted the need for more research to better understand which treatments work best for specific populations. However, many effective, evidence-based treatments are available. For example, cognitive behavioral therapy (CBT) for anxiety has shown additional benefit for comorbid disorders that impact children. Another effective treatment is exposure therapy, which not only helps to reduce symptoms of specific phobia, separation anxiety, generalized anxiety, and social anxiety but also provides more generalized benefits for decreasing comorbid anxiety disorders, Lewis said. Mindfulness-based treatment interventions are also increasing in popularity, she said, and have a growing evidence base for reducing anxiety and depressive symptoms in children. There is also evidence for the combined use of CBT and medication in certain populations. The Child/Adolescent Anxiety Multimodal Study showed that CBT and medication were effective interventions for separation anxiety, generalized anxiety disorder, and social phobias for some youth, but almost 50 percent relapsed (Compton et al., 2010; Ginsburg et al., 2018). It is important to consider ways to improve access to existing treatments to ensure that the "gold standard" of treatment is available to all children. Lewis mentioned two additional forms of therapy— interpersonal therapy (IPT), which has shown benefits for mood disorders and depression, and dialectical behavioral therapy (DBT), which has also been shown to reduce symptoms in young people with mood disorders and suicidal ideation. Overall, Lewis said, it is critical to take a person-centered approach, consider the SDOH that impact youth, and start with evidence-based treatments. When needed, evidence-based approaches can be modified to make them applicable and accessible to children from a variety of cultural and social backgrounds.

Emanuele called out the youth suicide crisis, emphasizing the increase in suicide rates for youth: it is the second leading cause of death for teens and young adults aged 10–34, with rates continuing to rise. Emanuele gave additional statistics to illustrate the scope of the problem. Twenty-two percent of high school students reported suicide ideation in the last year, with higher rates in female, LGBTQ+, and Indigenous populations. Ten percent of high school students reported suicide attempts in the past year, with higher rates (again) in female, LGBTQ+ and Indigenous youth, as well as Black youth. Emanuele said the COVID-19 pandemic had significant negative impacts on youth mental health, with increases in suicide rates among those aged 5–12 and 18–24 and increased rates of suicide by firearm during and after the pandemic. Additionally, self-injury rates increased post-pandemic, suggesting that it has increased, even in the absence of morbid intentions (CDC, 2023). Alvord provided information on risk factors and the impact of social media. She described how she engages in motivational interviewing with children, many of whom have suicidal ideation and comorbid mental health diagnoses. Alvord asked children what they value and what is important to them. She noted the importance of helping children understand the scope of their support system, highlighting the role of family, friends, and community. Alvord suggested using a prevention lens when considering suicidal ideation and behaviors, adding that it is important to reinforce the value of life. She noted risk factors known to increase suicide rates for youth, such as a family history of suicidal behaviors or severe mental illness, lack of access to resources, discrimination, economic poverty, and "not fitting in." Alvord shared known protective factors, including self-regulation, the ability to tolerate discomfort and disappointment, and the support of community, including schools, and social services. She closed by emphasizing the need for early detection for suicidal ideation in youth to connect them with resources and support as early as possible.

Emanuele asked Leonardo how parents and caregivers can support a child who is suffering from anxiety, depression, or other mental health disorder. Leonardo said it is helpful for them to have a basic understanding of anxiety and mood disorders, such as knowing about the risk factors, protective factors, SDOH, and potential contributors. They need to know where they can turn for supportive resources. Leonardo noted the many resources, books, and Internet trainings available, with information about how to support children with anxiety, and shared a list of resources from SAMHSA, Child Mind Institute, Childmind.org, the Jed Foundation, and the American Psychological Association. Leonardo highlighted a report entitled "American Psychological Association Health Advisory on Social Media and Teens (2023)"[14] (APA, 2023). She noted the importance of the caregiving role—providing a safe, consistent, nurturing environment; embracing holistic models to mental health promotions; and modeling self-care—and that having a sense of safety at home promotes mental health in children. Leonardo also suggested improving and deepening emotional relationships with children through quality time, encouraging emotional expression, active listening, being affectionate, and helping children develop skills such as problem solving, communication, and conflict resolution. Parents and caregivers should be considered part of the mental health "extenders" network that Monk and E. Carter referred to, Leonardo said. They can help to assemble a supportive community for their child, including extended family, coaches, teachers, faith leaders, and peers.

Finally, Leonardo said children should feel understood and embraced, adding that children with anxiety and mood disorders should know that their caregivers believe in their abilities and competence. Over time, these chil-

---

[14] See https://www.apa.org/topics/social-media-internet/health-advisory-adolescent-social-media-use (accessed June 17, 2024).

dren can increase their understanding of these disorders, access supports and resources, and develop and apply coping strategies.

POSTADOLESCENCE

The third session focused on women's mental health during the post-adolescence period[15] and was moderated by planning committee member George M. Slavich, professor of psychiatry and biobehavioral sciences, director of the Laboratory for Stress Assessment and Research, investigator at the Staglin One Mind Center for Cognitive Neuroscience, and research scientist at the Semel Institute for Neuroscience and Human Behavior at the University of California, Los Angeles (UCLA). The session featured presentations from Burnett-Zeigler, Eisenlohr-Moul, and Summer Mengelkoch, postdoctoral fellow in the Laboratory for Stress Assessment and Research in the Department of Psychiatry and Biobehavioral Sciences at UCLA, community partnerships workgroup chair at California State Trauma and Resilience Network, and visiting postdoctoral scholar in the Department of Genetics at Stanford University School of Medicine.

Slavich opened by stating that the developmental period of postadolescence is often a dynamic time. It is often spent juggling many responsibilities and identities that can include choosing partners and starting families. It is also a period when early-life vulnerabilities combine with an increase in life demands, stressors, and hormonal changes that can lead to preclinical issues and major health problems, Slavich said. Thus, the quality of care and services that women receive during this period is critical.

The Developmental Period of Postadolescence is Often a Dynamic Time: The Menstrual Cycle and Mental Health

Eisenlohr-Moul began by saying that despite the many reasons that women face an elevated risk of emotional disorders, her remarks would focus on the impact of ovarian steroid hormone fluctuations. She said that these begin around puberty and continue across the life cycle, through pregnancy and into menopause. They are correlated with increased risk for mental health disorders and symptoms, with the menstrual cycle functioning as frequent trigger of symptoms in women (Schiller et al., 2016). Adding to the complexity of the topic, Eisenlohr-Moul noted that most women do not experience negative mood or behavioral changes as a result of their cycle; however, for the minority who do, it can be devastating to their well-being. Figure 2 illustrates

---

[15] Postadolescence is defined as ages 18–34. See https://www.census.gov/library/stories/2017/08/young-adult-video.html (accessed June 13, 2024).

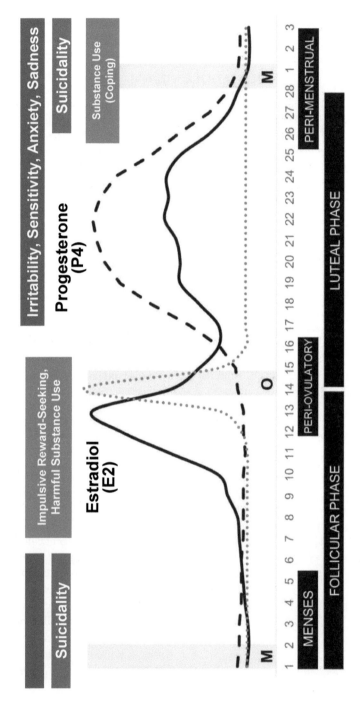

FIGURE 2 An overview of potential emotional and behavioral changes by phase of the menstrual cycle.
SOURCE: Presented by Tory Eisenlohr-Moul on April 29, 2024.

emotional and behavioral shifts that some women experience throughout the menstrual cycle. She emphasized the importance of acknowledging the consequences of hormonal shifts for those who are impacted, without creating harmful, misogynistic stereotypes by attributing these impacts to all women or cycling people.

Eisenlohr-Moul shared research illustrating that, for women who are sensitive to hormones causing mood disturbances, surges in progesterone are especially likely to trigger negative symptoms, including irritability, sadness, anxiety, and interpersonal sensitivity. She noted that irritability and sensitivity are the most common, with anxiety and sadness less dominant. Eisenlohr-Moul noted the elevated suicidality around menstruation and emphasized the complexity of hormone–mood interactions. The causes of mood disorders in women are extremely heterogeneous, Eisenlohr-Moul said. For example, one woman's depression could be triggered by estrogen withdrawal and another's symptoms by progesterone metabolites.

Another phenotype that Eisenlohr-Moul discussed was impulse and reward seeking (especially substance use) during ovulation, correlating with surges in estradiol. This has been a neglected phenotype due to stereotypes about mood changes in women focusing on the premenstrual time frame, Eisenlohr-Moul said. She suggested that a change of narrative is essential and urged further research on the multidimensional effects that hormone sensitivities can have during each phase of the menstrual cycle.

Eisenlohr-Moul discussed diagnostic criteria for hormone-related mood disorders (Epperson et al., 2012). She said that the sole diagnostic code is for premenstrual dysphoric disorder (PMDD), which was added to the DSM-5 in 2013 (APA, 2013). She noted that the diagnosis for PMDD is strict, requiring that a patient meet at least five diagnostic criteria (Gehlert et al., 2009). As a result, Eisenlohr-Moul said, only 5.5 percent of the female general population has been diagnosed with PMDD, emphasizing the point that not all cycling people have the distressing impact of variable hormones across the month. Eisenlohr-Moul noted that the diagnosis requires symptom tracking for 2 months, with noticeable mood differences consistently tied to changes in hormones (Kiesner et al., 2022). She emphasized that clinical cycle tracking can be difficult and labor intensive. In her clinical practice, Eisenlohr-Moul routinely sees women who experience an exacerbation of a mood disorder during hormonal shifts, but this situation does not qualify for a PMDD diagnosis. Research shows that among people with a depressive disorder diagnosis, 60 percent report some level of exacerbation around their cycle and during other hormonal shifts (Hartlage et al., 2004; Nolan and Hughes, 2022). However, they also do not meet the criteria for PMDD, because of the pre-existing diagnosis. Eisenlohr-Moul believes in a "silent epidemic" of untreated premenstrual exacerbation (PME), causing many women to experience hormone-related exacerbations of mental health conditions. She noted that PME may also contribute to misdiagnosis of bipolar disorder in women, without an appreciation of the role that hormones play in changing symptoms throughout the cycle.

Eisenlohr-Moul shared the potential burdens of living with PMDD. For example, women with PMDD find it hard to maintain personal relationships and employment (Halbreich et al., 2003). When someone is persistently irritable in unpredictable ways, she said, it can be devastating for personal and professional relationships (Hylan et al., 1999; Schmalenberger et al., 2017). She also highlighted the negative impact on children of having a mother or female caretaker who is prone to anger, irritable, and emotionally dysregulated. Women with PMDD also have an increased risk of suicidality, with 87 and 34 percent reporting suicidal ideation and a suicide attempt, respectively. Research has also found that a history of suicide attempts is associated with greater mood changes attributable to hormonal shifts, and some research has suggested that hospitalizations for suicide attempt peak during menstruation (Eisenlohr-Moul et al., 2022; Ross et al., 2024; Saunders and Hawton, 2006).

The final segment of Eisenlohr-Moul's presentation focused on potential treatments and the existing barriers to care for PMDD. Eisenlohr-Moul said that some evidence supports the use of selective serotonin reuptake inhibitor (SSRIs), either routinely or during the luteal phase only (ACOG, 2023). However, SSRIs have some potentially negative side effects, such as sexual dysfunction or sleep changes, which she said clinicians should discuss with their patients. Other approaches include drospirenone-containing oral contraceptives that suppress ovulation. This treatment has shown a smaller benefit than SSRIs, but it is FDA approved for PMDD and has been found to be more effective than a placebo in randomized controlled trials (RCTs). In cases of extreme PMDD, Eisenlohr-Moul said that some women choose chemically induced menopause, but this approach is not FDA approved.

Eisenlohr-Moul shared suggestions on how to improve mental health care services for women during hormonal shifts and transitions. She said there is insufficient training for health care providers on PMDD, PME, or hormonal mood changes in general. She pointed out that OB/GYNs are not trained to handle mental health concerns, and psychiatrists are not trained to handle hormonal issues. She called for additional research and training to help close this persistent gap in care. She also called for additional diagnostic tools and expanded diagnostic criteria and suggested that routine screenings could be incorporated into clinical care at certain points in a woman's life cycle, such as before major hormonal transitions. Finally, she called for an increased workforce of "mental health extenders." She closed by sharing the International Association for Premenstrual Disorder's website,[16] which includes more information for patients about the topic and training materials for clinicians.

Associations Between Hormonal Contraceptive Use and Depression

Mengelkoch spoke about the connection between hormonal contraceptive (HC) use and depression. She stated that her presentation aimed to make the case for "precision medicine" approaches that could change the way that women experience HCs and their mood-related side effects. She began by discussing these unintended consequences. Mengelkoch explained that HCs sometimes contain estradiol and always contain progestins. They are prescribed for many uses beyond preventing pregnancy, and more than 300 million women worldwide use them (Hill and Mengelkoch, 2023; Mengelkoch et al., 2024). About four in five U.S. women use HCs at some point during their reproductive life-span. Mengelkoch noted the more than 200 HC products on the market, including pills, patches, shots, implants, and intrauterine devices.

Although many patients believe that HCs have a localized effect, this is not the case. Hormones serve many functions and have receptors throughout the body, and the hormones in the HC can bind to these receptors and affect a wide variety of biological processes and behaviors. Estradiol and progesterone, both of which naturally occur in the body, influence sexual desire, inflammation, eating behaviors, reward reactivity, and mood. Mengelkoch noted that HCs have a broad safety profile and represent a revolutionary change for women, allowing them to control their fertility. However, Mengelkoch said, some experience negative side effects.

Mengelkoch said that mood-related changes are the most commonly reported side effect of HCs. However, the literature has mixed data on their role in depression, specifically. Mengelkoch noted several reasons for these inconsistent and unclear results, such as the various ages of users, varied duration of use, underlying genetic factors, pre-existing mental health issues, early-life stressors, overall physical health, and nutrition or dietary factors. Additionally, Mengelkoch reiterated the heterogeneity of HCs and suggested that the different hormone types, doses, and routes of administration may have an impact on side effects that is not captured by research approaches. Most research lumps all HC users into one group, rather than stratifying them by type, administration, or duration of use. A double-blind RCT that could result in an unintended pregnancy also has ethical issues. These challenges have led to numerous methodological issues, Mengelkoch said, as researchers rely on quasi-experimental studies, comparing users to nonusers, which makes it dif-

---

[16] See www.iapmd.org (accessed April 29, 2024).

ficult to prove causality. Additionally, it is not fully understood what factors may lead women to choose HCs and if these may play a role in depression risk. Mengelkoch also described the impact of "survivorship bias," meaning that the women in studies who take HCs represent a group who feel well enough to continue with them. Women experiencing the most severe side effects may cease use and not be represented in the research. Mengelkoch added that a lack of understanding of the etiology of depression further confounds the research on the relationships between HC use and depression risk and severity.

Mengelkoch reiterated that women are twice as likely as men to experience depression and that this risk is known to increase around major hormonal transitions, such as puberty, pregnancy, and menopause (Mengelkoch and Slavich, 2024). Mengelkoch also noted that although women experience more social and emotional stressors that may contribute to depression risk, research is also exploring the role of sex hormones in influencing that risk. Figure 3 illustrates overlapping mechanisms contributing to high rates of female depression.

Women on HCs have higher levels of c-reactive protein, a biomarker for inflammation, which puts them at increased risk for inflammation-linked

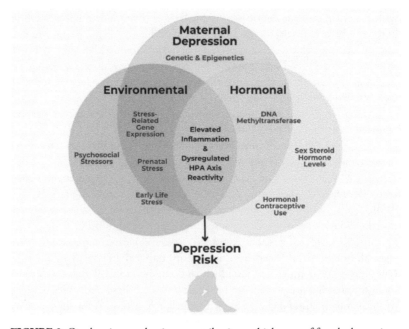

FIGURE 3 Overlapping mechanisms contributing to high rates of female depression.
NOTE: HPA Axis = hypothalamic-pituitary-adrenal axis.
SOURCES: Presented by Summer Mengelkoch on April 29, 2024; Mengelkoch and Slavich, 2024. CC BY 4.0.

diseases, both while taking HCs and afterward. Additionally, HC users have a blunted cortisol response to stressors. Both factors are associated with increased depression risk.

Mengelkoch's research examines both subjective changes in mood and the relationship between changes in cortisol levels and inflammation in women using HCs compared to women who were not (Mengelkoch et al., 2024). In HC users, as cortisol increased, their reported mood declined. Mengelkoch suggested that research exploring the unique intersection of hormones and stress response could better separate groups of HC users by administration type, duration of use, and other key differences.

Mengelkoch also described the benefits of a more precise approach to prescribing HCs that is rooted in individual risk assessment and includes ongoing symptom monitoring, especially for mood changes; users could be switched to an alternate form of contraception that might produce fewer negative unintended consequences. A barrier to precision prescribing is that most women are prescribed HCs by a general or family practitioner who is not an expert on the research on HCs or the options available. Mengelkoch suggested tools to overcome this barrier, such as precision medicine algorithms, or decision aid tools, which could help clinicians counsel their patients on HC choice and allow women to make more informed decisions from home.

Intersectionality of Social and Environmental Stressors and Mental Health

Burnett-Zeigler began by introducing the term "intersectionality," stating that it addresses the ways that "multiple forms of inequality or disadvantage compound themselves." She quoted the activist Kimberley Crenshaw, who is credited with coining the term, "Because the intersectional experience is greater than the sum of racism and sexism, any analysis that does not take intersectionality into account cannot sufficiently address the particular manner in which Black women are subordinated." Burnett-Zeigler noted that her presentation would focus on risk factors for developing mental health conditions in Black women and treatment considerations.

Burnett-Zeigler reiterated the complex ways in which SDOH factor into increasing risk for mental illness. Specifically, she noted exposure to racism, discrimination, acute and chronic stress (Alegría et al., 2013; Grote et al., 2007; Sibrava et al., 2019; Williams, 2018), and traumatic stress; lack of convenient access to health care; and lack of health insurance (Gwynn et al., 2008; Hasin et al., 2005; Kessler et al., 2003). Burnett-Zeigler said that these factors are especially salient in the lives of Black women, who face more housing instability, higher rates of domestic violence and trauma, higher rates of unemployment, and lower average incomes than White women. They are also more likely to be single mothers, which increases the stress and burden of caregiving and financial pressures, and to have higher rates of being uninsured, making access to quality care more challenging. Burnett-Zeigler noted that the high chronic stress, rates of trauma, and other SDOH also contribute to an elevated risk of other major health conditions in Black women, such as substance use disorders (SUDs), diabetes, cardiovascular disease (CVD), maternal morbidity and mortality, and negative birth outcomes[17] (CDC, 2017; Mukherjee et al., 2013; Petersen, 2019).

Burnett-Zeigler discussed the "weathering hypothesis," a framework coined by Arline Geronimus from the University of Michigan. It states that Black adults experience earlier health deterioration due to repeated exposures to social and economic adversity (Geronimus et al., 2006). "Weathering" includes biomarkers such as elevated blood pressure, cholesterol, and body mass index. Burnett-Zeigler noted that by age 45, 50 percent of Black women have a high weathering score that cannot be attributed to poverty alone. Burnett-Zeigler discussed cultural factors that may impact the health of Black women.

Burnett-Zeigler shared that many Black women have been cultured to "cope" with their suffering by presenting as strong and "masking" their real feelings. She noted that Black women who experienced more adverse child-hood experiences (ACEs) and felt the need to present an image of strength indicated more stress, anxiety, and depressive symptoms (Leath et al., 2022). It is important for clinicians and researchers to work with Black women within this context, she said, and connect them with needed resources, stated Burnett-Zeigler. Furthermore, research also suggests that Black adults have more negative attitudes and stigmatizing beliefs about mental illness and treatment and experience more shame and self-blame about seeking care, while also having higher levels of medical distrust, when compared to White counterparts (Brandon et al., 2005; Brown et al., 2010; Conner et al., 2010; Rusch et al., 2008; Tucker et al., 2013).

Burnett-Zeigler highlighted the mindfulness-based mental health inter-ventions that she uses as a psychologist in a community health center setting. She said her focus is "meeting Black women where they are." These inter-ventions have been shown to reduce symptoms of mental illness, including depression and anxiety, and improve general health, interpersonal relation-ships, and quality of life. They have also been shown to decrease blood pressure, improve heart rate variability, and improve inflammatory and immune response. Burnett-Zeigler stated that culturally tailored adaptations to empirically supported treatment approaches have been shown to be even

---

[17] See https://minorityhealth.hhs.gov/obesity-and-african-americans (accessed June 18, 2024).

more effective for ethnic minority populations (Bryant-Davis et al., 2024; Burnett-Zeigler et al., 2016; Jones et al., 2022; Neal-Barnett et al., 2011; Vroegindewey and Sabri, 2022). Although all of these programs are in pilot phase, have not been tested in an RCT, and need more research to fully elucidate their effectiveness, she noted that the guidelines from the Agency for Healthcare and Research and Quality for nonpharmaceutical management of depression recommend mindfulness-based interventions (AHRQ, 2009).

In closing, Burnett-Zeigler reiterated the importance of community engagement and relationships in achieving lasting impact. Community engagement and relationship building activities that are outside of a researcher's formal job description or research scope could play a key role in establishing the trust needed to conduct effective research and enable effective changes in care, Burnett-Zeigler said.

Discussion

Slavich asked the panelists to discuss best practices for translating research findings on how different patient populations respond to different treatments into effective clinical practice. Eisenlohr-Moul suggested centralized programs that increase clinician time with patients, require core patient assessments, and provide fair and sustainable reimbursement for the assessments. Mengelkoch expressed her excitement about the potential for technology-driven decision- making tools. She agreed with Eisenlohr-Moul about the benefits of a more centralized system but said that such tools could be a helpful first step. Burnett-Zeigler noted the benefits of clinicians considering the whole person, including SDOH. She also called for health care providers to be more aware of prevalence rates of certain illnesses in their populations and use that awareness to inform diagnosis and care. Eisenlohr-Moul added that doctors are limited by time constraints and the lack of health care system incentives to spend adequate time with patients, and she encouraged broadening the conversation to include administration and payment strategies.

Mary-Frances O'Connor, associate professor at the University of Arizona, referenced breast cancer literature that indicate mother–daughter communications about breast cancer have lasting effects (Fisher et al., 2020). O'Connor asked if the same is true for PMDD, whether family history and mother–daughter communications about hormone-related mental health concerns impact outcomes. Eisenlohr-Moul replied that, because menstrual stigma dictates that female children should only discuss these issues at home, intrafamily communication about the menstrual cycle has a large impact on women's understanding of what is normal or abnormal. When a child's mother or sisters have a history of PMDD, familial messages to her often indicate that cycle-related mood dysregulation is normal and something all women experience—

and this may reduce the likelihood of treatment-seeking. However, when genetically related girls and women do not have cycle symptoms, a female child is more likely to hear messages that the cycle does not influence mood or the more accurate message that cycle-related mood changes are abnormal. She noted that broader communications about the role of hormones in mental health can influence one's perspective and experiences.

Monk described the need for more obstetricians and gynecologists to acknowledge that some women are particularly sensitive to HCs and need to offer alternative approaches for these individuals. Mengelkoch called for additional research to improve understanding of the impact of hormonal changes on the mind and the body. Eisenlohr-Moul highlighted a study on the evidence-based prescribing of oral contraceptives for PMDD (Rapkin and Lewis, 2013) and said that elevating such research could help shift the cultural narrative.

An online audience member asked how to distinguish between "normal," or expected, premenstrual syndrome (PMS) and PMDD. Eisenlohr-Moul said that these conditions exist on a spectrum, and research is ongoing to determine the boundary between normal and abnormal. The key consideration, she said, is clinical distress or impairment. Another online audience member asked about any overlap between PMDD and attention deficit hyperactivity disorder (ADHD), and Eisenlohr-Moul said that this is not yet known but that grants are evaluating it systematically. Lewis Johnson asked about the potential for combined therapies for PMDD symptoms, using mindfulness-based therapies. Eisenlohr-Moul stated that trials provide little evidence that mindfulness or CBT improves symptoms of PMDD, although they can improve impairment.

MIDLIFE AND MENOPAUSE

Laura M. Rowland, director of NIMH's Neuroscience of Mental Disorders and Aging Program, offered opening remarks, noting that midlife is accompanied by menopause-related changes and challenges and an increased risk of mental health conditions, such as mood disorders and anxiety. The goals of the session were to describe anxiety and mood disorders and other mental health conditions that occur in women during midlife, along with the applicable interventions and health care services. The session featured presentations by Stephanie Faubion of the Center for Women's Health at the Mayo Clinic; Rebecca Thurston, principal investigator of the Study of Women's Health Across the Nation (SWAN), Pittsburgh Foundation Chair of Women's Health and Dementia, professor of psychiatry, psychology, epidemiology, and clinical and translational science, and director of the Women's Biobehavioral Health Program at the University of Pittsburgh; and Hadine Joffe, interim chair of the Department of Psychiatry and executive director of the Mary Horrigan Connors Center for Women's Health and Gender Biology at Brigham and Women's Hospital, Harvard Medical School.

Menopause and Mental Health

Faubion began by providing background information on the epidemiology of menopause, followed by a discussion of mood concerns during it and an overview of relevant research. She said that menopause is defined as having no menstrual cycle for 12 consecutive months and that although the average age of occurrence is 52, it varies, with 90–95 percent having reached menopause by 55. About 5 percent of women experience menopause at 40–45, and a small minority of women, 1–3 percent, will do so before 40. The time leading up to menopause, called "perimenopause," can last for 6–10 years and presents with a variety of symptoms, many of which mimic those of menopause. Perimenopause lasts until a woman reaches menopause.

Faubion noted more than 30 symptoms associated with menopause, the most common of which are hot flashes, sleep disturbances, vaginal dryness, joint pain, genitourinary issues and incontinence, cognitive dysfunction, and mood changes (Avis et al., 2015; Gartoulla et al., 2015; Harlow et al., 2022). Hot flashes are experienced by about 75 percent of women, for a mean duration of 7–10 years. Women who begin to have symptoms during perimenopause may have them for even longer. Faubion said that racial and ethnic differences have been found in the prevalence and severity of menopause symptoms, with hot flashes tending to start earlier and last longer in Black (Freeman et al., 2014) compared with White women. The symptoms also tend to be exacerbated by obesity (Freeman et al., 2014), Faubion noted. These symptoms are associated with reduced quality of life, sleep problems, negative mood, and physical health conditions, such as decreased bone density, elevated heart attack and stroke risk, and heart failure (Freeman et al., 2014). Hot flash severity is associated with lower educational attainment, higher rates of ACEs, smoking, and obesity. For some women, Faubion said, hot flashes persist even after age 65.

Faubion discussed the Hormones and ExpeRiences of Aging study conducted at four Mayo Clinic sites (Faubion et al., 2023). The questionnaire examined how many days of work women missed due to menopause symptoms, whether and how they reduced their workload, if they were fired or quit, or if they had retired or changed jobs. Faubion said that the mean number of missed days attributable to menopause symptoms was three per year. Using U.S. Census Bureau data for employment and income for women aged 45–60, she estimated that such missed work and income loss totals $1.8 billion annually. If medical expenditures are included in these costs, Faubion said, the estimation jumps to $26 billion.

Faubion discussed the connection between menopause severity and the burden of caregiving. She said women make up an estimated 61 percent of U.S. caregivers and that the average female caregiver is 49 years old.[18] Women are also more likely to be in charge of the care of two or more adults. These midlife, female caregivers fall into what is referred to as the "sandwich generation," Faubion said, as they may be raising children and caring for aging parents (and often also balancing a career). This double burden is a chronic stressor, with an association between the number of "caregiving hours" and the severity of a woman's menopause symptoms. Research shows that symptom burden is directly correlated with caregiving hours per week, and this persists even when adjusting for possible confounders such as self-reported psychological health issues (Saadedine, 2023).

Faubion detailed the sleep disturbances and mood changes that are hallmark symptoms of menopause. She said that one in four women experience insomnia, and women are 40 percent more likely to have insomnia than men (NIH, 2005). Faubion also highlighted that perimenopause is a window of vulnerability for depressed mood or a major depressive episode for all women, not merely those with a history of depression (Brown, 2024; Maki, 2019). However, women with a history of depression are at greatest risk for worsening depressive symptoms during this period. Risk factors include a previous episode of depression, antidepressant medication usage, a diagnosis of anxiety or PMDD, and sociodemographic factors, such as being Black, stressful life events, and social isolation.

Faubion said that the first line of treatment for mood disorders in this population is a combination of CBT and antidepressants. She noted the importance of monitoring any side effects from pharmacological treatments and adjusting medications. It may also be possible to use estrogen therapy, Faubion said, to manage depressive disorders in perimenopause. Estrogen has been shown to have a similar magnitude of benefit as antidepressants when administered to perimenopausal women with depression. She said that the data on causes and treatment for anxiety are mixed, but elevated anxiety may be linked to elevated vasomotor symptoms (VMS), such as hot flashes, and reducing anxiety may reduce those as well.

Faubion described her research using the Data Registry on Experiences of Aging, Menopause, and Sexuality dataset. It involves more than 16,000 women who completed questionnaires about their menopause symptoms. In one analysis, women with severe hot flashes were twice as likely to have obstructive sleep apnea, and Faubion noted that any woman reporting severe hot flashes should be screened for sleep apnea in a clinical setting. Women who

---

[18] See https://www.caregiver.org/resource/women-and-caregiving-facts-and-figures/ (accessed June 13, 2024).

reported poor sleep quality were also 1.5 times more likely to report sexual dysfunction, and those who reported the highest-quality sleep also reported the most sexual activity. Another important point was a connection between ACEs and menopause symptom severity, highlighting the benefits of clinically screening women for ACEs as part of routine menopause care, Faubion said (Faubion, 2018). Faubion concluded by urging increased attention to menopause from the research community, given its impact on half of the global population.

SWAN

Thurston's presentation focused on the results of SWAN,[19] a longitudinal cohort study of 3,302 women across five racial and ethnic groups who were recruited in the mid-1990s at ages 42–52, experiencing perimenopause or menopause at recruitment. The goals of SWAN, Thurston said, are to characterize the natural history of the menopause transition, test its antecedents and health consequences, and compare the experiences of women across racial and ethnic groups. She noted that although the study is formally on menopause, it also examines female aging more broadly.

Thurston explained that menopause is marked by a shift in hormones—in general, estradiol decreases, and follicular stimulating hormone increases (Randolph, 2011). However, Thurston and Faubion also noted the wide variability in the specific magnitude and patterns of hormone changes women will experience. Thurston shared data on racial/ethnic differences in VMS—hot flashes and night sweats—experienced by a majority of women during the menopause transition. She said that the most frequent, severe, and persistent symptoms were found in Black women and the least frequent in Chinese and Japanese women (see Figure 4).

Thurston said SWAN identified a correlation between VMS and sleep. Sleep problems increase during perimenopause and continue to worsen through late perimenopause and early menopause. They include trouble falling asleep and staying asleep, middle-of-the-night wakings, and early-morning wakings. The most common menopausal sleep issue is middle-of-the-night waking (Kravitz, 2017). SWAN has found that women with more frequent VMS have more sleep problems (Kravitz, 2017). She noted that the mechanisms underlying the relationship are unclear, but her research with the MsHeart Study with objective measures of both sleep and VMS found a marked increase in wakings during or immediately after a hot flash (Thurston et al., 2019).

Thurston detailed the presence of depressive symptoms and disorders during midlife, presenting data from SWAN showing that women have an

---

[19] See https://www.swanstudy.org (accessed June 13, 2024).

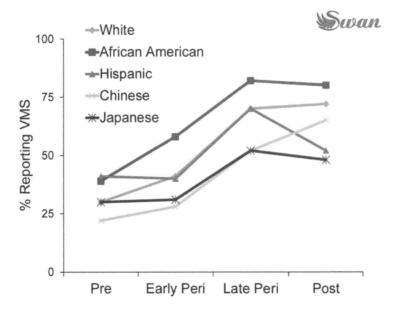

FIGURE 4 Vasomotor symptoms (VMS) by race/ethnicity during various stages of perimenopause.
SOURCES: Presented by Rebecca Thurston on April 29, 2024; Gold et al., 2006.

almost doubled risk of elevated depressive symptoms during the early post-menopause and that anxiety symptoms are also common. The SWAN Mental Health Study also found that women experience a 2–4-fold increased odds of a major depressive episode during late perimenopause and early postmenopause. Results indicated that 52 percent of women had at least one major or minor depressive episode during the 13-year follow-up period. The study did not find a strong correlation between hormone levels and depressive symptoms or disorders. The strongest risk factor for depression was history: the majority (59 percent) of women with a history of depression experienced a depressive episode during the transition. Other risk factors included financial stress, VMS, poor sleep, and concurrent medical conditions (Bromberger, 2011).

Menopause is a "biopsychosocial" transition, said Thurston, describing the optimal future of menopause care as collaborative care between medical and behavioral health providers. Close friendships were found to buffer against this rise in depression during menopause, highlighting the importance of community and social connection. Empirically supported therapies to treat mood and anxiety disorders include CBT, DBT, IPT, and other mindfulness-based approaches.

In closing, Thurston said that midlife can be a time of increases in personal growth and well-being; the Midlife in the United States study finds that women, but not men, experience an increase in positive affect and life satisfaction in their 50s and 60s. Thurston asserted that positive elements of midlife aging can also be harnessed to help women transition through and grow during this important stage of life.

Depression in the Menopause Transition

The final speaker was Joffe, who focused on depression during the menopause transition, illuminating the causal factors and potential pharmacologic and hormonal therapies. She said that although every female individual will go through menopause and its change in hormones, not all will experience depression. "That's really critical because as an individual approaches perimenopause, we want them to feel empowered… to feel that they have the education they need to approach this stage of life and to appraise their risk as best as possible," Joffe said.

Joffe explained the difference between major depressive disorder (MDD) and subthreshold depression, stating that the latter is more likely during the menopause transition. She said that "Sleep is critical for any phase of mood disturbance at any stage of life" and reiterated that sleep fragmentation, or interruption of sleep in the middle of the night, is the typical sleep disturbance during the transition. She noted that subthreshold depressive symptoms are closely linked with sleep fragmentation and MDD more linked with problems of falling asleep and overall lack of sleep.

In her research, Joffe found that nighttime hot flashes and sleep disturbance contributed to mood changes and that progesterone was protective against mood problems, which supports the recent FDA-approved medication, allopregnanolone (ALLO), which is produced from progesterone and used to treat postpartum depression (Gordon et al., 2018; Joffe et al., 2019; Schweizer-Schubert et al., 2020). The decrease in ALLO may decrease feelings of calm and elevate excitatory neurotransmission, contributing to depressive feelings and anxiety (McEvoy and Osborne, 2019). Joffe noted that she is conducting research to investigate the inflammatory, neuroprotective, and sleep mechanisms involved in this phenomenon during perimenopause.

Joffe also spoke about the importance of translating research into useful therapies. Potential treatments for menopause-related depression include hormonal therapies (Gleason et al., 2015), conventional psychiatric medications, novel compounds, and behavioral approaches (Dias et al., 2006; Joffe et al., 2007). Of the nonhormonal treatment options, Joffe said that SSRIs and serotonin norepinephrine reuptake inhibitors (SNRIs) have been shown to be effective. She said that neurokinin antagonists, one type of novel agent, have not been tested in trials for menopause-related depression, but they have been shown to improve quality of life in some women with hot flashes (Simon et al., 2023). She said that research on novel therapeutics for anxiety and mood-related symptoms during the transition will be key to the future of menopause care. Menopause-specific CBT holds promise for mild symptoms, she said, but no data yet show a benefit for more severe menopause-related MDD. Joffe said that hormonal therapies are most useful and effective when the dominant symptoms are VMS (Gordon et al., 2018; Joffe et al., 2001; Kornstein et al., 2010, 2014a,b; Morrison et al., 2004; Schmidt et al., 2000; Soares et al., 2001, 2003).

Discussion

Rowland opened by asking where women should turn for support with their varied menopausal symptoms, noting that collaborative approaches may not be accessible to all women. Thurston said the type of care sought first should be reflective of the dominant symptom. For example, if that is VMS, then the best provider would be a gynecologist. Ideally, Thurston recommended seeking a health care provider with training in menopause care, who could be a primary care provider, gynecologist, or psychiatrist. She noted that the Menopause Society has a directory of health care providers[20] who are trained in menopause-specific care. Faubion agreed and noted that many gynecologists and primary care providers do not know how to manage menopause symptoms. She said that this fragmentation of care is costly to the health care system. Faubion called for both clinician and patient education regarding the relationships among menopause symptoms and potential treatments. Faubion noted that most medical residents only get 2 hours of training on menopause during their entire medical education. Thurston concurred, adding that the lack of menopause training even applies to those specializing in obstetrics and gynecology.

Inger Burnett-Zeigler asked Thurston about what might account for the elevated VMS symptoms observed in Black women in SWAN. Thurston said that the racial differences could not fully be explained by the available SWAN data but noted that socioeconomic factors and stress, including race-related stressors, were likely partial contributors. Black and financially stressed women also reported poorer-quality sleep, Thurston said, which will exacerbate the experience of the menopause transition.

Clark asked how practitioners can keep up with the evidence base on effective treatments. Thurston acknowledged that many challenges exist in

---

[20] See https://portal.menopause.org/NAMS/NAMS/Directory/Menopause-Practitioner. aspx (accessed June 13, 2024).

translating research into effective care options. Thurston and Faubion suggested that research and clinician education opportunities would be useful to integrate best practices for menopause management into clinical care.

Galambos asked about consumer education strategies. Faubion noted the importance of both disseminating useful information and combating misinformation. Thurston agreed and highlighted the role of medical societies in providing the public with accurate and easy-to-understand information. Faubion suggested that women should be informed about potential symptoms starting at age 35, before they begin to experience them. She provided an anecdote of a patient who had major concerns about her symptoms, including heart palpitations, panic attacks, night sweats, and hair loss, unaware that these could all be related to her menopause transition. Thurston noted that there is less consumer education on symptoms related to menopause than for other life stages, such as menarche and pregnancy. She reiterated the point made by Joffe: knowing what to expect can help shift a woman's perception of her symptoms and experience of the menopause transition.

HEALTHY APPROACHES TO MENTAL HEALTH AND AGING

A session on healthy approaches to mental health and aging was moderated by Charles F. Reynolds, distinguished professor of psychiatry and emeritus endowed professor in geriatric psychiatry at the University of Pittsburgh School of Medicine (UPSM). The session featured presentations from four speakers: Carla Perissinotto, professor of medicine at the University of California, San Francisco; Carmen Andreescu, professor of psychiatry at UPSM; O'Connor; and Helen Lavretsky, professor in residence at UCLA. The speakers covered essential mental health topics, such as loneliness and the role that it plays in depression, connections between depression and dementia, the emotional burden of prolonged grief, and whole-person methods for building mental health resilience.

Loneliness and Isolation in Women

Perissinotto spoke about the ways that social isolation and loneliness are associated with chronic illness in women, including anxiety and mood disorders. Perissinotto defined key terms, stating that loneliness is a subjective feeling of being alone; it is the distress that a person experiences when they do not have the relationships that they want. Social isolation, on the other hand, is an objective measure of the quantifiable number of relationships (e.g., family, friends, and the community). These two concepts are distinct, but they interact and coexist in meaningful ways (see Figure 5). Social connection, a broader term, exists on a spectrum and encompasses loneliness and isolation or

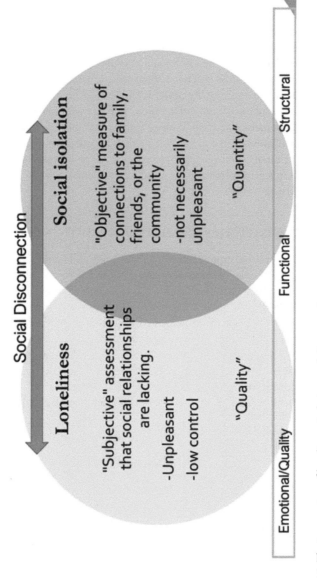

FIGURE 5 The intersection of loneliness, isolation, and disconnection.
SOURCE: Presented by Carla Perissinotto on April 29, 2024, adapted from Korwal et al., 2021.

can be understood by examining the structure, function and quality of social connections. However, the ways to address them and their consequences are different.

Perissinotto explained that during the COVID-19 pandemic lockdowns, loneliness became a popular topic. In February 2020, the National Academies released a report on the health consequences of social isolation and loneliness in older adults (NASEM, 2020), which became highly relevant to the national dialogue. A year later, the surgeon general issued an advisory, raising concerns about the public health implications of loneliness and isolation.

Perissinotto shared data on the prevalence of social isolation and loneliness across the life-span, with a focus on aging. Using 2012 data from the Health and Retirement Study, Perissinotto found that 43 percent of people over 60 reported some degree of loneliness (Perissinotto et al., 2012). Other studies in the United Kingdom found that 10 percent of older adults suffer from chronic or severe loneliness, and social isolation impacts one in four people (Cudjoe et al., 2020; Hawkley et al., 2022; Perissinotto et al., 2012; Victor and Bowling, 2012).

Perissinotto discussed the known risk factors for loneliness and their impacts on women. She said that societal trends have moved away from connection, with time spent with family, friends, and community decreasing (Kannan and Veazie, 2023). Losses are also key predictors of loneliness, especially later in life, including the death of a spouse or close friend, the loss of physical health or mobility, and changes to living arrangements. Women experience a higher risk for loneliness than men, due to a variety of factors (Aartsen and Jylhä, 2011), Perissinotto said, including that more women than men are caregivers, and caregivers have a higher risk and prevalence of loneliness. U.S. women have a longer life expectancy, making them more likely to lose a spouse, higher rates of urinary incontinence, leading to social isolation and loneliness, and history of abuse and trauma, which can increase risk of social isolation and loneliness (Dykstra et al., 2005; Newall et al., 2014; Nicolaisen and Thorsen, 2014; Tijhuis et al., 1999; Victor and Bowling, 2012; Wenger and Burholt, 2004).

An especially high-risk group that Perissinotto highlighted is female veterans of the armed services. She noted that female veterans have higher rates of loneliness[21] than their male counterparts, attributable to both their experiences in the military and the unique challenges of returning to civilian life. "Women warriors" report that their identity as a veteran significantly affects their social health, often keeping military and civilian friends separate.

Perissinotto illustrated the connection between loneliness and depression by saying loneliness is an experience, not a diagnosis, but there are known

---

[21] See https://newsroom.woundedwarriorproject.org (accessed June 13, 2024).

overlaps between the two concepts (Barger et al., 2014; Burholt and Scharf, 2014; Domènech-Abella et al., 2017; Hughes et al., 2004; Lewis et al., 2023; Peerenboom et al., 2015). She suggested that loneliness be conceptualized as SDOH, noting that it can co-occur with depression and anxiety, and the relationships are complex and bidirectional. A person with depression may withdraw socially, for example, precipitating the cycle of loneliness, isolation, and depression. Perissinotto et al. (2012) found that people over 60 who experienced any amount of self-reported loneliness also had an increased risk of mortality (Perissinotto et al., 2012). These results have been validated by other studies, she said (Barnes et al., 2022). Perissinotto noted some methodological concerns in the research, including a lack of distinguishing between social isolation and loneliness in some studies, but said results still broadly echo the surgeon general's warning about the negative health impacts attributable to loneliness.

Another impact of loneliness, Perissinotto said, is the growing incidence of "polypharmacy," or the use of numerous medications for a growing list of symptoms. She noted that people who are lonely and isolated often perceive their symptoms of pain, anxiety, and insomnia as more severe. As a result, patients are prescribed additional medications, which carries both physiological risks and economic implications. One analysis estimated that social isolation among older adults costs the Medicare program $6.7 billion per year.[22]

Perissinotto said that the long-term impacts of societal shifts toward smaller family sizes and less time spent with friends and community are unknown. Additionally, although data show that older adults who are LGBTQ+ face higher risk of loneliness and social isolation, data are lacking for racial/ethnic populations or other marginalized groups—particularly around how to intervene. Perissinotto also expressed the need for additional research on strategies to prevent the development of loneliness across the life-span.

In closing, Perissinotto reinforced that loneliness is an adaptive feeling and a reminder of the human need to connect with others. The problem, she said, arises when the feeling becomes maladaptive, and one cannot find ways to connect and experiences stress and anxiety as a result. Loneliness is a public health issue to be tackled at a policy level, Perissinotto said.

The Dark Triad: Depression, Anxiety, and Dementia

Andreescu introduced the dark triad, which refers to syndromes that are interconnected through multidirectional relationships; depression, anxiety, and dementia are highly correlated, and the directionality goes both ways.

---

[22] See https://www.aarp.org/pri/topics/health/coverage-access/medicare-spends-more-on-socially-isolated-older-adults.html (accessed June 13, 2024).

Late-life depression, Andreescu said, is a highly recurrent disease with a significant socioeconomic burden. It increases disability, mortality, and risk for metabolic disease, cognitive decline, and suicide. She said the elevated risk for depression in women continues into late life, and treatments for late-life depression are only moderately effective. Fewer than half of individuals respond to first-line treatments, and of those who do, many relapse or recur within 4 years (Andreescu et al., 2019). Research aims to identify early markers of treatment response, Andreescu said.

Andreescu described her research from 2017, in which functional brain networks in patients aged 65+ were examined before and after pharmacological treatment for depression over 12 weeks (Karim et al., 2017). Brain scans indicated a significant difference after just 1 day of treatment between the people who did and did not respond. There were also distinct sex differences. These baseline changes were viewed as predictors of treatment response in male patients but not observed in female patients (Wilson et al., 2023). Her ongoing research[23] has shown a difference between people who were never depressed and people who have late-life depression when examining functional connectivity networks. Depressed participants who maintained remission did not look like those who had never been depressed, and depressed participants who relapsed had more similarities to people who never had depression than those who maintained remission. The theorized hypothesis for these findings is that remitted depressed participants acquire a new homeostasis that keeps them less vulnerable to new stressors. Furthermore, she added that white matter hyperintensity volume[24] is associated with higher risk of recurrence and white matter[25] tracts integrity is likely important to functionality. A rigid structure of damaged white matter tracts may pose a problem for healthy, adaptive brain function.

Andreescu drew the connections between late-life depression, anxiety, and cognitive decline. She said that some clinicians in dementia care view anxiety as a mild, prodromal symptom of dementia. However, as a geriatric psychiatrist, she sees the relationship between dementia and anxiety as bidirectional. Much of the data on anxiety in older adults suggests that it is dramatically underreported. Older adults are more likely to report "concern" or "stress" and less likely to use the word "anxiety," which may be seen as stigmatizing, Andreescu said. She said that women and older adults are more likely to attri-

---

[23] Gerlach, A. R., H. T. Karim, A. Kolobaric, B. D. Boyd, K. Kahru, R. T. Krafty, O. Ajilire, W. D. Taylor, and C. Andreescu. Network homeostasis: functional brain network alterations and relapse in remitted late-life depression. (under review)

[24] White matter hyperintensity volume is a measurement of the size of legions in the brain's white matter that appear hyperintense on magnetic resonance imaging.

[25] White matter is found in the deeper tissues of the brain.

bute anxiety symptoms to a physical illness rather than perceiving them as generalized anxiety (Andreas et al., 2017; Beekman et al., 2000; Forlani et al., 2014; Golden et al., 2011; Kertz et al., 2012; Lee et al., 2023; Wolitzky-Taylor et al., 2010). A 2020 study including more than 29,000 people examined the link between anxiety and dementia and showed that anxiety symptoms were significantly associated with increased risk for all-cause dementia and especially Alzheimer's disease. Worry, one of the anxiety phenotypes, is associated with higher levels of amyloid and tau proteins, which are known to be associated with dementia (Donovan et al., 2018; Lavretsky et al., 2009; Pietrzak et al., 2012; Pietrzak et al., 2014; Santabarbara et al., 2020).

Andreescu's lab also examined brain age using machine learning to analyze gray matter density (Karim et al., 2021). Using the Penn State Worry Questionnaire (PSWQ) and rumination subscale from the Response Style Questionnaire, they studied the impact of worry and rumination on brain health and found that for every point increase on the PSQW scale, a brain appears to be 1.3 months older by brain age rating. Another study examined the relationship between anxiety and hippocampal volume (Karim et al., 2024). The hippocampus is known to be impacted by dementia and one of the earliest affected areas in Alzheimer's disease. The research showed that worry and rumination are correlated with reduced volume. Conversely, people who were able to reframe negative experiences had healthier hippocampal structures into old age.

Andreescu concluded by reiterating the complex relationship between depression, anxiety, and dementia and noted that depression and anxiety independently raise dementia risk through multiple pathways. She also said that physical health is key to brain health and that as physical health deteriorates in late life, it can strain the vascular system, which affects brain function. Physical ailments, such as diabetes and high blood pressure, Andreescu said, raise a person's risk for late-life depression.

Prolonged Grief Disorder (PGD): A Mental Health Disorder Distinct from Depression

O'Connor spoke about PGD and how it uniquely impacts women later in life due to a variety of social factors. It is characterized by persistent, intense grief that interferes with functioning, exceeds the expectations of the person's social, cultural, or religious groups, and lasts for at least 12 months after the initial loss, according to the DSM-5 definition. PGD is associated with an increased risk for suicide and other negative health consequences, such as cancer and CVD. It is distinct from typical acute grief in many ways, and O'Connor noted that suffering due to bereavement is a normal part of the human experience, but PGD occurs when the intensity and frequency of waves of grief do not change over time, which is the typical pattern seen in grieving, she said.

O'Connor stated that "bereavement is a health disparity," with women bearing much of the burden. Women are more likely to be widowed; by age 65, nearly 40 percent are widowed compared with 13 percent of men (West et al., 2014). O'Connor also reiterated that women are more likely to be caregivers (Pinquart and Sörensen, 2006), and added that the self-neglect and poor mental health that can occur during long periods of caregiving predicts the development of PGD (Lenger et al., 2020). She explained that the bereavement burden is exacerbated among women in communities of color, because marginalized communities have higher mortality rates; multiple deaths in a family or a community increase their bereavement load (Donnelly et al., 2022; Lewis et al., 2021). In the United States, Black people have a life expectancy that is 6 years shorter, on average, than White people and higher rates of infant mortality. Furthermore, O'Connor illuminated negative health impacts unique to Black women: losing three or more people has been shown to increase cardiometabolic risk (Lewis et al., 2021). In addition to the emotional toll of bereavement, it has financial and social repercussions, and women and people of color experience these most acutely (Greenman and Xie, 2008), O'Connor said.

Using three patients as case studies, O'Connor illustrated some key facets of PGD. The first was a middle-aged woman who said, "why would I give my daughter a bat mitzvah when their grandmother isn't here to see it," suggesting that a major life event no longer held any meaning, due to the loss of a loved one. The next patient was a woman in her 20s who said that after her loss, she would never be able to enjoy listening to music again. This response showed that a numbness and meaninglessness had entered her life, which is a hallmark symptom of PGD. The third patient was a woman who had been a pillar of her community, but after her son was shot and killed, she felt that she could no longer hold space for other people's problems. She felt anger and bitterness, hallmark symptoms of PGD.

O'Connor distinguished PGD from MDD and PTSD. While fear is a hallmark of PTSD and undifferentiated sadness is a hallmark of MDD, PGD emphasizes yearning, longing for the person who is gone, and wanting to be with them, unable to face the new reality. PGD predicts a higher risk of suicide, due to the person's desire to be with the person that they lost.

O'Connor also distinguished "grief" from "grieving." She said that grieving is a long-term process, and grief is experienced and measured in the moment. Grieving can be thought of as a form of learning, she said, as the brain needs to relearn the world without a relationship it had come to depend on. She noted that grieving is the way that grief changes over time and that if measures of grief have not changed by 12 months, a person is more likely to develop PGD.

O'Connor discussed her research on the neurobiology of PGD. A 2008 study showed that it is related to reward-related brain functions rather than the impact of a stressful life event (O'Connor et al., 2008). The study examined self-reported feelings of yearning and activation scans of the nucleus accumbens (NA) region of the brain. Those diagnosed with PGD showed increased activity in it compared with those who were typically grieving. She noted that with disruption of homeostatic reward mechanisms in the brain due to a disruption in the bond with a parent, child, partner, or other close relationships, yearning and prolonged grief may result.

O'Connor also reviewed the evidence-based treatments for PGD. She stated that antidepressants are not effective for PGD unless depression is also present. O'Connor said that three RCTs funded by NIMH, showing a benefit for "PGD therapy," which involves CBT combined with exposure therapy (repeated references to the loved one being gone) (Shear et al., 2005, 2014, 2016). She noted that the exposure therapy component is critical to the benefit, which was not seen with CBT alone (Bryant et al., 2014).

O'Connor concluded by reiterating that PGD is a clinical disorder that goes beyond the normal process of grieving. She said that knowledge of PGD is low, even among health care professionals, with a critical shortage of clinicians who are trained in evidence-based treatments for it. This shortage, she said, is driven in part by the excess deaths attributable to the COVID-19 pandemic, as well as the opioid epidemic (Kumar, 2023). O'Connor said that more and better research is needed to fully understand the grieving process and training to enable clinicians to better support people with PGD; although evidence-based treatments exist, they are underused. She suggested that bereavement therapies be tailored to communities and reiterated the disproportionate impact of grief and bereavement on women and communities of color.

Holistic Approaches for Women's Mental Health

Lavretsky focused on holistic approaches to caring for women in late life living with mental disorders, referencing the concept of "whole-person health" (NASEM, 2023). Lavretsky said that individual responses to stress are shaped by exposures to trauma and abuse; major life events; environmental stressors, such as work, home, and community safety; and behavioral factors, such as tobacco use, alcohol use, diet, exercise, and sleep. Although most people can withstand some stress, when it becomes chronic, the response can become maladaptive. Lavretsky said that the aging brain is vulnerable to external stressors, as it carries a burden of chronic inflammation, potential vascular disease, and neurodegeneration; when combined, these factors can culminate in depression, anxiety, or cognitive decline. However, protective factors include social support, physical and cognitive activity that help build brain reserves, providing an opportunity to build resilience to stress and prevent or reverse the mental disorders of aging (Weisenbach and Kumar, 2014).

Resilience refers to the ability to recover from adversity and stress, Lavretsky expanded. It considers brain neuroplasticity and neuroprotection and mental, emotional, cognitive, and physical health. She said that the most established ways to boost resilience are improving sleep, diet, and exercise and reducing stress with mind–body interventions. She listed resilience-building interventions: psychotherapy, learned optimism training, hardiness training, focusing on the positive aspects of difficult experiences, and spiritual practices.

Lavretsky discussed the role of holistic, complementary, and integrative treatment approaches and highlighted the popularity of mind–body therapies, such as tai chi, yoga, and biofeedback (Johnson et al., 2019). Manual therapies, such as massage and chiropractic spinal manipulation, are increasingly popular as well, she said, as are traditional and alternative medicines, such as Ayurveda and Traditional Chinese Medicine. Lavretsky detailed the research supporting these therapies and noted evidence gaps for some. Women and White people tend to use integrative therapies more than men and other racial/ethnic minorities.

For anxiety and depression, Lavretsky said, interventions such as animal support therapy have been shown to increase endorphins, dopamine, and oxytocin and to decrease cortisol. Music therapy reduces depression and anxiety and enhances well-being, with ongoing research studying its impact on brain health. Movement therapies, such as dance and yoga, improve mood and sleep by modulating serotonin and dopamine, and aromatherapy stimulates the olfactory bulb and modulates the limbic system, reducing stress and agitation. Light therapy and melatonin have been reported to be effective for sleep and mood. Generally, these modalities have no adverse side effects, and Lavretsky invited those interested to find more information through the National Center for Complementary and Integrative Health.[26]

Lavretsky gave examples of complementary and alternative practices to manage menopause-based mood and cognitive disorders, such as vitamins, mind–body practices, and "social support practices" (Chiaramonte et al., 2017). She said that herbal supplements and vitamins—such as phytoestrogens, black cohosh, red clover, Vitamin B6, and Vitamin D3—have all had some evidence supporting positive effects on well-being, as do mind–body practices, such as yoga, tai chi, qigong, and hypnosis, although more research is needed. Lavretsky said that comprehensive human flourishing—including mental, emotional, social, environmental, and spiritual well-being in individuals and communities—should be the goal of healing practices. She suggested

---

[26] See https://www.nccih.nih.gov/ (accessed June 20, 2024).

focusing on brain health as the foundation, because optimal brain health optimizes mental health (Eyre et al., 2023), as well as emotional and physical health. One way to support brain health is adequate sleep, and Lavretsky noted that 7–9 hours of sleep is essential for proper cognitive function, reduced depression and anxiety, and reduced anger and aggression. Sleeping allows the brain to clean and organize itself, she said, as does physical exercise. According to the American Heart Association, research supports 150 minutes of moderate exercise and 2–3 days of weight training every week to improve the integrity of the blood–brain barrier, regulate microglia, reduce amyloid plaque, which is associated with Alzheimer's disease, and reduce neuroinflammation (ACC/AHA, 2019; Arnett et al., 2019). Diet can also support inflammation reduction and brain health, and Lavretsky noted that research supports the use of diets such as the Mediterranean, Dietary Approaches to Stop Hypertension (DASH),[27] and Mediterranean Intervention for Neurodegenerative Delay (MIND) diets for reducing depression and improving cognition up to 30 percent, compared to the standard U.S. diet (van den Brink et al., 2019). Dietary and lifestyle factors, when used to support overall health and reduce stress, have been shown to reduce morbidity, reduce polypharmacy, benefit vascular health, reduce chronic inflammation, reduce telomere attrition, change epigenetics, and improve mitochondrial function. Lavretsky emphasized that a more holistic approach to health could reduce health care spending and improve the lives of millions of women.

Lavretsky detailed her research on "The Pink Brain Project," which studies yoga as a therapy for women at high risk for developing Alzheimer's disease. All subjects were postmenopausal women, over age 50, with subjective cognitive decline. They all had one or more CVD risk factors, including high blood pressure, diabetes, or high cholesterol. The participants were randomized to receive either kundalini yoga training or standard memory training for 12 weeks with 24-week follow-up. Lavretsky noted that kundalini yoga was chosen for its gentle nature and ability to be done while sitting in a chair, due to the age and health status of the research participants. Mood and memory were measured alongside subjective quality-of-life measures, biomarkers, such as inflammatory markers, and neuroimaging. They found that the yoga intervention showed reductions in CVD and vascular disease risk, and memory training did not. The yoga intervention also led to reduced anxiety and forgetting. Memory training improved verbal recall, but the brain scans showed that although the memory training group lost gray matter during the course of the 2-year study, the yoga intervention increased gray matter. Although inflammation markers rose in the memory training group, the yoga intervention saw inflammatory markers stabilize. Both groups saw increases in brain connectiv-

---

[27] See https://www.nhlbi.nih.gov/education/dash-eating-plan (accessed June 20, 2024).

ity, but in different regions, including hippocampal regions. Lavretsky noted that similar findings with a tai chi training intervention have occurred in other studies of older adults with depression (Kilpatrick et al., 2022). Older adults seem to respond well to mind–body interventions, showing increased brain connectivity, neuroplasticity, reduced depression and anxiety, improved cognition, and increased psychological and emotional resilience, she said.

In closing, Lavretsky asserted that a whole-person approach to health produces positive results, improves lives and brain health, reduces health care costs, and can have real clinical applications for women's health. She noted that research could address multicomponent interventions to treat and prevent mood and cognitive disorders in women. As an example of a best practice, she shared that the Veterans Health Administration system is working with patients to provide comprehensive, whole-person care that improves quality of life.[28]

Discussion

First, Lewis Johnson asked if mind–body interventions are equally effective when practiced in a group or alone. Lavretsky noted that this difference has not yet been quantified, but practicing in a group that increases social support has benefits versus individually. She also noted the ongoing research to compare in-person and virtual yoga interventions.

Joy Burkhard, founder and executive director of the Policy Center for Maternal Mental Health and planning committee member, asked the speakers to address the psychotic symptoms that can accompany cognitive decline. Andreescu said that some forms of dementia include psychotic symptoms, but others do not. For example, Lewy Body Dementia is often associated with visual hallucinations, and Alzheimer's often includes psychotic symptoms, especially in the later stages. She noted that anxiety can also increase in the early stages of dementia and decrease in the later stages. Perissinotto added that many patients have psychotic symptoms due to polypharmacy or poor prescribing practices. These symptoms often resolve when medications are removed or properly managed, she said.

Reynolds asked about an intervention that could be administered early in the grieving process to prevent PGD. O'Connor said that social isolation may contribute, because people who feel alone in their grieving may find it more difficult to restore a meaningful life. She said that research could help determine whether community support, or peer support, could forestall PGD.

Eisenlohr-Moul asked O'Connor about the differences between PTSD and PGD, and O'Connor referenced research showing there are populations

---

[28] See https://www.va.gov/washington-dc-health-care/programs/whole-health/ (accessed June 20, 2024).

with comorbid PTSD and prolonged grief. However, each diagnosis seems to involve a distinct brain process; for example, orbitofrontal activation occurs in PGD (a reward-related region) but not PTSD (Bryant et al., 2021). PGD shows NA activation, which is associated with craving, yearning, and wanting lost loved ones to return.

EXPLORING POLICY OPTIONS

The second day of the workshop began by considering systemic, federal policy solutions to benefit women experiencing anxiety and mood disorders and address barriers to access and gaps in knowledge for women's mental health care. The session was moderated by Fields Allsbrook and featured a discussion with panelists Burkhard; Jocelyn Frye, president of the National Partnership for Women & Families; Beth Carter, senior policy advisory at the AARP Public Policy Institute; and Katie Russo, vice president of business development and operations at the Anxiety and Depression Association of America. The conversation explored several themes, including challenges with fragmented care, low reimbursement rates, and research gaps.

Fields Allsbrook began by broadly asking the panelists about notable gaps in knowledge or practice in women's mental health care for which effective policy is lacking. Burkhard replied that low reimbursement for mental health care providers and a lack of in-network providers to serve specific patient populations, such as those on public insurance, is a common concern. An additional challenge that receives less attention is the costly administrative burden of health care operations, particularly impacting community health centers and other safety-net providers. Burkhard noted an opportunity to develop infrastructure to reduce this burden. For example, one solution would be for an outside entity to assist with organizing and executing administrative tasks, such as billing. Another fundamental issue Burkhard described is that mental health has become siloed and viewed as separate from physical health. It is often not covered by standard health insurance; it is carved out through separate provider and patient contracts, despite the bidirectional connections between mental and physical health. There should not be a need for mental health parity laws, Burkhard said, because these fields should never have been divided.

Frye added that another fundamental issue is the racial disparities in maternal health and health care. This is a problem for which broad-scale solutions are lacking, she said. She referenced comments made by speakers who emphasized the opportunities of integrated care teams, working across practices, and creating an extended network of mental health care providers and advocates. She posited that policy might be used to improve patient knowledge of available resources, such as connecting women who visit a prenatal care provider to mental health resources. Frye also noted the importance of reducing stigma surrounding the topic of mental health care, especially in certain patient populations, such as Black women. She noted that women living in communities of color may be less likely to seek support with mental health conditions, due to pervasive stigma. Frye said that gaps in access to care for women is not a new problem but rather a long-standing challenge that requires continued investment.

Russo said that better marketing and communication, and harnessing technology and digital tools, could help to improve patient outreach, communication, and education. Technology allows for expanded reach of information about mental health services, which can improve public knowledge of their existence, and thus, ability to access resources. B. Carter added that policy development should be evidence based, which she noted is challenging in women's and geriatric health, given that women and older adults have been excluded from research and clinical trials. She said the representation is key to improving policy development and suggested that policy makers fund research on the intersectionality of age, gender, and behavioral and physical health to support developing tailored, culturally appropriate screening tools and diagnostic criteria. Beyond developing the evidence base, B. Carter said that policy makers can continue to support developing, testing, and evaluating effective, integrated health care models to improve access to care. She specifically suggested developing and promoting holistic, person-centered primary and behavioral health care.

Fields Allsbrook asked how stigma and bias impact the effectiveness of policies and programs to support women's mental health. Burkhard said that maternal health care providers, midwives, and obstetricians and gynecologists should provide mental health screenings routinely. However, the lack of common practice perpetuates stigma around mental health care. She said that such screenings should be as common and necessary as screenings for gestational diabetes, for example. Frye added that bias is a barrier, because women may be perceived as sensitive, nervous, or anxious and thus not have their concerns taken seriously. These stereotypes impact access to proper diagnosis and care, a challenge that is more pervasive with women of color, including Black women. Furthermore, research suggests that Black women experience perceived discrimination in clinical settings and are not taken seriously (Njoku et al., 2023).

Russo reiterated Burkhard's comment that mental health is viewed as separate from physical health, leading to a scenario in which someone can visit a doctor and have a long list of physical health concerns addressed but never receive support for depression, for example. She suggested all health care providers be informed of the impacts of untreated mental health illnesses and become equipped with the tools to screen and refer for mental health care. B. Carter suggested that policy makers fund grants and initiatives to support, strengthen, and diversify the mental health workforce. She said that more than 163 million people in the United States live in areas with shortages of mental health providers, and more than half of rural counties lack psychologists, psychiatrists, and social workers (Belz et al., 2024; Strong et al., 2023). Mental health care access will depend on growing this workforce, B. Carter said.

Fields Allsbrook asked the panelists about potential policy solutions related to SDOH. Frye began by saying that society relies on women for unpaid labor, often as caregiving for both children and aging populations, which creates an excessive stress burden. Frye shared her experience as a caregiver for her parents with cancer and the challenges of balancing the extra workload on top of her career. Economic ramifications and growing inequities run downstream from this unpaid care burden, Frye said. She added that caregiving is commonly viewed as women's responsibility, limiting women's perception of it as a stressor or burden. She noted that these factors contribute to a health care system riddled with barriers to women's health.

Burkhard added this is a unique time in the nation's history to examine SDOH. There is a new urgency following the Supreme Court decision overturning *Roe v. Wade*, which has led to bipartisan support of pregnant and postpartum women and young families. She noted that this presents an opportunity to advocate for policy changes, such as subsidized child care and paid leave, that could support those groups, referring to a bipartisan committee in Congress that is discussing paid leave policies. She said that research supports paid leave for both men and women, enabling men to be more engaged in their children's lives from the beginning and also framing caregiving as a family issue. She pointed out that under animal welfare laws, dogs are not allowed to be separated from their puppies for at least 6 weeks, but no similar laws exist for human mothers and their babies. This example highlights the importance of updating maternal health policies that reflect a basic understanding of maternal and infant welfare, Burkhard said.

Fields Allsbrook invited the panelists to share promising solutions at the federal, state, or local levels. B. Carter said policies that support integrating behavioral health into primary care have made huge strides. In addition, federal mental health parity acts mandate health insurance plans cover mental health and substance use disorder (SUD) services at levels comparable to medical and surgical services. However, additional progress could help to ensure true reimbursement parity. For example, she noted inconsistencies in the law's application and that Medicare is not subject to it. Additional funding for coordination, monitoring, and enforcement across multiple agencies would support full implementation of the law, she said.

Frye noted that many states are expanding access to Medicaid for at least 1 year postpartum, which has been an important step forward for maternal health. Additionally, 14 states and the District of Columbia require access to paid family leave. These are improvements, but this would ideally happen at the federal level, Frye said. Burkhard noted that mental health could be more fully integrated into pregnancy care. She added that it is important to expand the maternal health workforce and that the federal government could create a strategic plan for addressing clinician shortages. One option, she said, would be to create maternity care centers that provide holistic services, such as access to both midwives and obstetricians, strategically located in maternity care "deserts." She emphasized that this approach could be foundational to reducing maternal care disparities. She also suggested growing a workforce of peer support specialists, for which all 50 states have state-sanctioned training and certification programs. Peer support is commonly used for SUD interventions, but it could have broader applications for mental and maternal health. She said that developing this workforce falls under the purview of HRSA, adding that HRSA could also provide support for care providers located in health care deserts and community health centers to enable them to become Medicaid eligible, reducing their reliance on grants and temporary programs. Fields Allsbrook and Russo echoed the call for collaborative and coordinated care across various types of health care providers and for government funding to train providers and the public in the practice of this form of care. Lack of coordination and education leads to suboptimal care and poor outcomes, Fields Allsbrook and Russo said.

Fields Allsbrook concluded by asking the panelists how to ensure that policy solutions for mental health programs are inclusive of all women, regardless of age, race, ethnicity, or gender identity. Russo again called for representation in policy development. Frye added that "women cannot be an afterthought" and that it is important to center the voices of women in all steps of policy development. She added that centering the needs of the most marginalized in society generally improves the lives of everyone. She also suggested that policy makers partner with community members for concrete policy solutions and not just "their stories" and lived experience. Communities can articulate what they need, Frye said. Burkhard and Frye called for investment in infrastructure and broad, systemic health care reform. For many of the challenges discussed during the workshop, an evidence base directly points to solutions, but these are not being implemented. Burkhard said that the challenge is not that we do not know what to do but rather implementation. She noted that we need more implementation science—focusing on the role of payors, including creating and distributing billing codes for all evidence-based care, measuring delivery of it, and focusing on quality improvement initiatives to improve delivery of it. She added that some recommendations from the United States Preventative Services Task Force[29] and HRSA's Alliance for Innovation on Maternal Mental Health[30] could be shifted to mandates on both payors and providers, giving the example of the recommendation of screening for maternal depression. She reiterated the importance of finding ways to adequately reimburse providers for this screening and monitoring, noting that most obstetricians receive a flat-rate payment for all prenatal and birth-related care, which does not incentivize them to screen or spend additional time with their patients for treatment planning and follow-up care. In closing, Fields Allsbrook noted that evaluations often assess the "average" care, but the care provided to women, people of color, and people with disabilities is often below average—a challenge that could be better addressed through disaggregated health care evaluations and quality measures.

Discussion

Perissinotto asked about how to improve access to care while acknowledging challenges in primary care, including financial and administrative challenges. Russo suggested that nonprofits working in mental health care collaborate with primary care health professionals and clinics to provide resources. She also added that nonprofits often compete for funding and attention but could function more effectively as collaborators, and Frye concurred. However, Burkhard pushed back on the idea that nonprofits should take on more responsibility for informing patients about which providers in their area are qualified to support them. She noted that nonprofits exist as a result of gaps in infrastructure and government systems. The many mental health nonprofits should be a signal of the grand failure of the federal government to address mental health; it must take on a larger role by expanding mental health education and requiring such training as component of medical education and training.

O'Connor addressed the topic of women as unpaid caregivers, noting that the COVID-19 pandemic highlighted many challenges with a system that relies on so much unpaid care. She asked how unpaid caregiving could be better addressed in future discussions of pandemic preparedness. Frye responded that research from the Center for American Progress has shown that the economic costs of unpaid caregiving during the pandemic was about $600 billion.[31] However, society is suffering from "pandemic amnesia," she

---

[29] See https://www.uspreventiveservicestaskforce.org/uspstf/ (accessed June 20, 2024).

[30] See https://mchb.hrsa.gov/programs-impact/programs/alliance-innovation-maternal-health (accessed June 20, 2024).

[31] See https://www.aarp.org/pri/topics/ltss/family-caregiving/valuing-the-invaluable-2015-update.html#:~:text=In%202021%2C%20the%20estimated%20economic,value%20of%20%2416.59%20per%20hour (accessed June 20, 2024).

said, and has yet to implement the lessons learned, including those related to the benefits of paid time off for caregiving, community-based services, and child care. She noted that although issues such as caregiver support, child care, and mental health care are connected, advocacy for each is siloed.

Clark asked the panelists for their thoughts on Medicaid coverage of doula services. Burkhard said that despite some coverage, it is often difficult to bill. She added that coverage for postpartum doula care would also be beneficial, especially for single mothers, mothers of multiple children, and those with a history of postpartum depression. Fields Allsbrook added that Medicaid reimbursement for doulas rarely provides a living wage, and it is often not covered by private insurance, noting additional areas for improvement. Monk proposed developing a student loan forgiveness incentive program for care providers who accept Medicaid and provide mental health services to marginalized populations.

Fields Allsbrook closed the session by reiterating the roles of multiple groups, including clinicians, nonprofits, community members, and patients, in solving health care system challenges for effectively delivering care services for the women's health.

SPECIAL POPULATIONS

Fields Allsbrook pivoted to the next segment of the policy discussion, featuring Alex Sheldon of GLMA: Health Professionals Advancing LGBTQ+ Equality, Kimberly Aguillard of Mathematica; and Nicolle L. Arthun of Changing Woman Initiative and Transcending Strategies LLC. The presentations highlighted the experiences of the LGBTQ+, disability, and Native American communities, through the lens of advocates and researchers within these communities.

The LGBTQ+ Community

Sheldon discussed the many challenges facing the LGBTQ+ community in terms of mental health, discrimination, and access to medical care, and the lessons that could be applied to improving policy and care provision. Sheldon explained key terms, such as "nonbinary," "cisgender," "transgender," and "gender dysphoria," which they described as "the feeling of psychological distress that might occur for someone who is transgender." They also noted the large variance in how it is experienced.

Sheldon said that mental health disparities are especially high in transgender people, who face four times the risk of depression compared to the general population. Studies also show that 80 percent of transgender people have contemplated suicide, and they have higher rates of SUD, ADHD, autism spectrum disorder, and other forms of neurodivergence. Sheldon highlighted that these issues are exacerbated for LGBTQ+ community members who also belong to communities of color or other historically marginalized groups.

Sheldon introduced an LGBTQ+ think tank, the Movement Advancement Project,[32] that tracks LGBTQ-related policies across all 50 states (see Figure 6). The map illustrates the extent to which a state's policies protect or harm the health and livelihoods of LGBTQ+ persons. Sheldon noted that states depicted in green had proposed legislation that, overall, was favorable or protective of LGBTQ+ communities, and states depicted in red had proposed legislation that is mostly discriminatory toward or harmful for LGBTQ+ people.

Sheldon also noted that as LGBTQ+ communties are not monolithic, policies impact different segments in varied ways. For example, although lesbian, gay, and bisexual populations have gained rights in recent years, transgender people have lost rights. Sheldon highlighted state and regional differences in accessing care for members of the LGBTQ+ community, noting the pervasive existence of care deserts, or "care apartheids," so labeled because they are human-made systemic forms of oppression. Sheldon noted that some state Medicaid programs actually prohibit coverage for transgender care.

Sheldon spoke about anti-LGBTQ+ legislation introduced in 2023, stating that it was the worst year on record for transgender rights. Approximately 700 bills were introduced in state legislatures, most of which were intentionally harmful for transgender individuals. Sheldon said that these bills addressed four main topics: health care, protection in schools, sports participation, and identifying document laws. Sheldon focused on the laws pertaining to health care, noting the harm on LGBTQ+ persons by limiting access to, or criminalizing, gender-affirming care. They said that the majority, possibly as high as 90 percent, of transgender youth live in states with some level of ban on access to gender-affirming medical care. This shift has also occurred alarmingly quickly, Sheldon said, with five times as many attempts to criminalize transgender medical care in 2023 as in any prior year. Sheldon stated that GLMA provides legal challenges to laws that aim to prohibit care and is engaged in lawsuits against North Carolina, Missouri, and Texas. Sheldon suggested that many of the same groups aim to limit both access to health care for transgender individuals and women's bodily autonomy.[33]

Sheldon discussed how the need for ongoing defense erodes the mental health of LGBTQ+ individuals and communities. They said that the political environment is hostile toward LGBTQ+ individuals, with debates over whether transgender people deserve to be treated as human beings. This

---

[32] See https://www.lgbtmap.org/equality-maps (accessed June 15, 2024).

[33] See https://www.lgbtmap.org/equality-maps (accessed June 14, 2024).

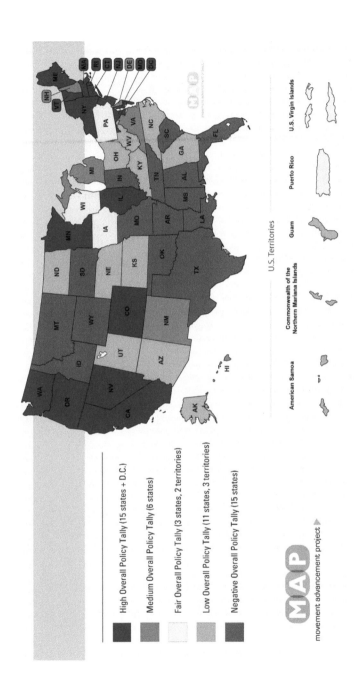

FIGURE 6 Equity Maps Snapshot: LGBTQ Equality by State Data as of April 30, 2024.
SOURCE: Presented by Alex Sheldon, April 30, 2024. Movement Advancement Project. See https://www.lgbtmap.org/equality-maps (accessed June 14, 2024).

climate exacerbates feelings of marginalization, fear, and invalidation for this population along with chronic stress levels, anxiety, and depression. According to the Trevor Project,[34] 86 percent of transgender or nonbinary youth said that the recent debates over anti-LGBTQ+ legislation had negatively impacted their mental health. School hate crimes against LGBTQ+ people have also increased, quadrupling in recent years in states with anti-LGBTQ+ laws. Health care providers are at risk as well; clinicians who care for this population have also reported receiving threats. Sheldon closed by highlighting the importance of advocacy, and specifically of health care providers joining LGBTQ+ advocacy groups, to generate public interest in the topic. They invited audience members to join GLMA and gain access to on-demand continuing education trainings on the culturally competent provision of LGBTQ+ health care.

Women and Girls with Disabilities

Aguillard spoke about lessons learned from the disability community to address barriers to mental health care access. She began by affirming her personal identity within the community, noting that she is blind and thus provides the perspective of both a researcher and a person with lived experience. Although disability can be defined in many ways, the definition in the context of federal nondiscrimination laws states that it is a substantial limitation in one or more major life activities.[35] She said these limitations can be physical, cognitive, or sensory—noting that the latter include sensitivity to light, sound, smells, and textures—which can impact the ability to focus or communicate. Aguillard provided statistics on disability in the United States, stating that one in four people lives with a disability, and it is more common in certain populations, such as those over 65, American Indian and Alaska Native (AI/AN) people, non-Hispanic people, and women (Manning et al., 2023).

Aguillard said that people with disabilities are three times more likely to live in poverty than those without disabilities (CAP, 2015), and women with disabilities experience higher rates of poverty, lower employment, and lower wages compared to men with disabilities. This disparity may be partially due to women balancing employment with caregiving and household demands, on top of their disability. Women with disabilities also face social pressure and marginalization and experience violence that is rooted in pervasive social discrimination, sexism, and ableism (Aguillard et al., 2022). Aguillard noted

---

[34] See https://www.thetrevorproject.org/ (accessed June 14, 2024).

[35] See https://www.ada.gov/topics/intro-to-ada/ (accessed June 20, 2024).

some risk factors for mental health issues, including negative stereotypes and experiences related to people assuming incompetence in those with disabilities; ableist microagressions; and employment, health care, education, and social discrimination (Dunn, 2019). All of these factors, she said, can compound, impacting self-esteem, stress, anxiety, and other mental health conditions. Aguillard described the isolating experience of being the only blind woman who has ever worked for her company, in every job she has had. She noted that people with disabilities face the possibility of being abused by caregivers, and ever-present communication barriers prevent people with disabilities of various forms from fully participating in society.

Aguilar described other critical barriers. Government health insurance programs, which cover many people with disabilities, often lack comprehensive coverage, requiring the person to prioritize the costs of physical health care, leaving limited funds for mental health care (Manning et al., 2023). Furthermore, transportation is often more costly, particuarly in rural communities, and there is a higher prevalence of people with disabilities in rural areas. Aguillard said that, despite the passage of the Americans with Disabilities Act more than 33 years ago, many buildings are not fully wheelchair accessible. Many websites are not equipped with assistive reading technology, and videoconferences frequently do not have captions. Tele-mental health can also lack accessibility options for enabling communication, navigation, and interaction. Mental health providers may not be familiar with relay services for people with hearing or speech disabilities or resources for providing sign language interpreters.

Aguillard shared that medical providers are often focused on the physical needs of people with disabilities and struggle to focus on mental and emotional needs. Additionally, health care providers often stereotype or infantilize them. Clinician bias can cause long-term harms to both the patient–clinician relationship and patient care (Dunn, 2019). Aguillard said research shows that people with disabilities value being able to work with a care provider who shares their disability to avoid these barriers (Mogensen and Hu, 2019). Testing environments are often not conducive to people with sensory disabilities, potentially leading to incorrect diagnoses, she added.

To address some of these challenges, Aguillard said resources should be allocated for research and accessibility programs that address the mental health challenges of people with disabilities, especially women. She also suggested that efforts to diversify the mental health workforce should include people with disabilities. She said that only 2 percent of psychologists report having a disability. Training to reduce disability stigma should be required for clinicians, and both physical and digital mental health care environments and technologies should be designed and built with accessibility in mind, she concluded.

Indigenous Women's Mental Health

Arthun provided background information and challenges experienced by Indigenous populations related to mental health care. The United States has 574 federally recognized AI/AN tribes, and two-thirds of Indigenous individuals do not live on reservations. She noted that half of the AI/AN population is women, and 26.6 percent of AI/AN people live in poverty, which is nearly twice the national average. Nearly one in five (19 percent) of people who identify as AI/AN reported having a mental illness in the past year (MHA, n.d.).

Arthun described economic, structural, and geographic barriers in accessing care. With higher rates of poverty and a lower median income, Indigenous populations may find that affordable mental health care is out of reach. Additionally, Indigenous individuals are more likely than the general population to be uninsured, and those with insurance are often covered through Medicaid or the Indian Health Services (IHS). IHS services are administered on the reservations, which are not where the majority of Indigenous populations live. Some individuals must drive multiple hours to access care through IHS.

Despite comprising only 1.3 percent of the overall U.S. population, Arthun said, AI/AN people make up 10 percent of the homeless population, and housing in tribal communities may also have deficiencies related to heating, plumbing, or a lack of running water. She also noted that the majority of Indigenous communities are in the rural Midwest or Western regions and suffer from "health care deserts."

Arthun described the overlapping issues of mental health and maternal mortality among Indigenous women. She said that 14–30 percent of AI/AN women experience maternal depression (Policy Center for Maternal Mental Health, 2023). They also report higher rates of depression than White women and higher rates of anxiety than other women. She stated that 93 percent of AI/AN maternal deaths are considered preventable, and these are most commonly attributed to hemorrhaging or mental illness (Policy Center for Maternal Mental Health, 2023). Many social inequities and the burden of systemic racism are contributing factors, Arthun said. Rates of IPV are also higher for Indigenous women, which also contributes to higher rates of PTSD. Arthun desribed her experience as a midwife, seeing countless women with past trauma, sexual abuse, or childhood abuse who had developed anxiety or PTSD and had often not been properly diagnosed or treated (Policy Center for Maternal Mental Health, 2023).

Arthun referenced recommendations from the Advisory Committee on Infant and Maternal Mortality[36] to help address these challenges. She noted

---

[36] See https://www.hrsa.gov/advisory-committees/infant-mortality (accessed June 16, 2024).

the importance of universal screening and surveillance for IPV in the evaluation of all pregnant and postpartum individuals, such as the Pregnancy Risk Assessment and Monitoring System survey. Arthun suggested that the maternal mortality review committees review all deaths—including homicides, suicides, and overdoses—during pregnancy and up to 1 year postpartum. She also noted that the National Violent Death Reporting System Database of the Centers for Disease Control and Prevention could include pregnancy and IPV fields in surveillance measures.

Arthun shared that Indigenous women are more likely to seek out traditional healers than Western doctors, adding that Indigenous women are generally uncomfortable in clinical settings and often feel unsafe during talk therapy. "Creating a safe space means making sure that the location and the space feels comfortable...hogans, dirt floors, and fireplaces, and sage and cedar...actually create a lot of safety and feeling of comfort," said Arthun. She suggested traditional Indigenous healing or traditional chinese medicine as a more appropriate alternative. She also suggested better assessments of patient readiness and noted the negative stigma related to prescription drug use in the Indigenous communities.

In closing, Arthun noted the importance of improving living conditions for Indigenous mothers and infants and expanding access to health care. Other suggested strategies include improving funding for IHS and conducting reviews of its maternal care services and facilities to ensure high-quality maternal and infant care. She also called for expanding Medicaid access for Indigenous communities, especially for those who do not live near IHS facilities. Arthun suggested that IHS could be improved by integrating more traditional healing practices into its Western care model, noting that health care providers could benefit from additional training on strategies to support patients with a history of trauma, as many Indigenous women are trauma survivors. Arthun encouraged focus on improvements in communication and the creation of a safe, supportive health care environment for Indigenous women.

Discussion

Burnett-Zeigler asked Sheldon if GLMA had data on mental health outcomes for 2022–2023, during the increase of anti-LGBTQ+ legislation. Sheldon said not yet but noted that GLMA has population data on reactions to these bills at the state level and the effects on transgender lives, including stress, anxiety, and depression. Eisenlohr-Moul asked Sheldon about inclusive language and how to discuss sex and gender in the context of women's mental health. Sheldon said inclusion matters, as well as the understanding that sex and gender "are far more diverse than we really pay attention to." They also stated the need for a concerted effort to include LGBTQ+ persons in data and research to fully capture the needs of this population. They emphasized the need to offer gender-affirming care and said that women's health equity cannot be achieved without eradicating transphobia. O'Connor asked Arthun to describe her experience with the fraudulent residential treatment centers targeting Indigenous communities to receive reimbursement from Medicaid, often called "sober living homes."[37] Arthun said that communities are mobilizing to protect themselves and do not rely on government or federal agencies to protect them.

IMPROVING CARE PROVISION

Nima Sheth with the Advisory Committee for Women's Services at SAMHSA introduced this session by reiterating the many roles and stressors experienced by women and highlighted structural challenges in the health care system. She also suggested better integrating health systems with an understanding of the social and structural determinants that impact the health of women. Sheth said the Maternal Mental Health Task Force prepared a national strategy for Congress,[38] but many of the recommendations have yet to be implemented. Sheth also introduced the panelists for this session: planning committee member Heidi Nelson of the Kaiser Permanente Bernard J. Tyson School of Medicine; forum member Kirsten Beronio of the Center for Medicaid and CHIP Services; and Ayo Gathing of Humana, Inc.

Implementing Screening Guidelines for Anxiety, Depression, and IPV

Nelson spoke about implementing screening guidelines for anxiety, depression, and IPV through the lens of a pilot program that aimed to inform the Women's Preventive Services Initiative[39] and the HRSA guidelines.

Nelson described WPSI as a coalition of national health professional and patient advocacy organizations with expertise in women's health. She noted that it began with the National Academies consensus report on women's preventive services (IOM, 2011). WPSI reviews evidence, develops recommendations, and follows a methodology similar to the U.S. Preventive Services Task Force, she said. Its goal is to fill gaps in health care recommendations. If its recommendations are adopted, the services are required to be covered by most

---

[37] See https://azmirror.com/briefs/hobbs-arizonans-should-be-outraged-at-the-sober-living-home-scandal/ (accessed June 20, 2024).

[38] See https://www.samhsa.gov/sites/default/files/mmh-strategy.pdf (accessed June 20, 2024).

[39] See https://www.womenspreventivehealth.org/ (accessed June 20, 2024).

payers with no copay or deductible charges for patients as provided under the Affordable Care Act. Nelson added that screening for depression, including in pregnant and postpartum people, is covered under the Affordable Care Act and part of standard practice.

Nelson explained the two areas of research highlighted in the pilot study. WPSI recommended screening for IPV and anxiety in 2010 and 2020, respectively. She noted that depression, anxiety, and IPV can coexist and often go undetected, or misdiagnosed, for a variety of reasons. Routine screening for all three can help to identify the underlying causes of various physical and mental health symptoms. Nelson noted that detecting underlying mental health symptoms can significantly impact clinical management practices and patient health outcomes.

The pilot program first examined EHRs of patients for evidence of anxiety and IPV screening to identify eligible participants and conducted semistructured interviews. They found a wide variety of practices, numerous challenges with both knowledge and practice, and that screening rates were low and not well documented in the EHR. Screens for depression were more common than anxiety and IPV but often inaccurately conflated with anxiety screenings. Nelson also noted that health center staff were unaware of the recommended referral practices for patients who screen positive for anxiety or IPV.

Nelson's team examined the barriers and facilitators to conducting anxiety and IPV screenings in urban and rural health centers using 28 semistructured interviews across 12 clinical sites. One key facilitator was the ability to leverage current screening practices. Another facilitator was universal screening for all adults, which removed the conceptual barrier of deciding whom to screen. Barriers Nelson noted included screening fatigue, concerns about documenting and reporting while protecting patient confidentiality and safety, and difficulties discussing sensitive topics, such as IPV.

Next, resources were developed to support routine screening linking clinicians to screening tools, assessment, and billing codes, as well as Spanish versions for each resource.

Clinical screening workflows that included algorithms, screening instruments, and reference material were developed for clinics. Nelson said that the intention was for the materials to provide evidence-based resources to guide appropriate referrals for patients. Overall, the response to the materials was positive, noting them to be useful and supportive of patient and clinician needs. Some clinicians were overwhelmed and did not know how to operationalize the tools. Additional concerns that clinics expressed pertained to billing, coding, and documenting the use of the screenings. Nelson said that primary care clinics want to be involved in supporting women's mental health, but they require tools, information, and support. Nelson stated that training and implementation of the screening tools will be key next steps.

Improving Access to Mental Health and
SUD Treatment and Support Services

Beronio spoke about recent improvements by the Centers for Medicare & Medicaid Services (CMS) for accessing mental health and SUD support services. She explained that Medicaid is a partnership between state and federal governments. At the federal level, levers incentivize state agencies to participate in certain programs or extend coverage to specific conditions. However, coverage is ultimately determined primarily at the state level, she said.

Beronio discussed actions by CMS to improve provider network adequacy within Medicaid. She said CMS recently issued rulings around the maximum allowable wait time for an appointment. This was intended to address access challenges for specific services, such as mental health care, primary care, and obstetrics and gynecology. She said that the maximum allowable wait time is 15 days for primary care and obstetrics and gynecology and 10 days for mental health and SUD appointments. To ensure compliance, a provision for "secret shopper" surveys is in place to validate that states are meeting standards.

CMS is raising the required Medicaid reimbursement rate for health care providers, Beronio continued, which also aims to allow nonmedical care providers to be reimbursed. She also discussed actions by CMS to strengthen implementation of mental health parity requirements, including ways to make the requirements for documentation less burdensome, while still ensuring that accountability in reporting is maintained (CMS, 2023).

Beronio said that CMS is focused on innovation to improve integration and collaboration. She described collaborative care as clinicians from various backgrounds working together to deliver mental health care support, alongside nonmedical care providers. She noted that changes were made in Medicaid policy in 2023 to allow states to pay for specialist consultations within a primary care office, allowing primary care physicians to offer more options to patients and streamline access to care. CMS also supports telehealth to increase access to care. She noted that CMS supports EHRs but cannot finance a full transition to an EHR system.

One CMS priority noted by Beronio is increasing health care access for youth. CMS requires states to cover all care that is deemed "medically necessary," and since 2022, CMS has been working to add mental health and SUD care to that list, to expand and improve access across states. CMS has also awarded grants to states to pilot the use of Medicaid in school-based settings and produced new guidance on how to file claims for these services, Beronio said.

Other CMS priorities are supporting maternal and mental health, Beronio stated. She noted that 45 states have accepted new plan options to extend Medicaid coverage for women for at least 1 year postpartum. CMS is also working to expand crisis response capacity, including helping states to improve access to mobile crisis response teams. CMS offers federal match dollars of up to 85 percent for states to build a mobile crisis unit and is working to draft additional guidance on the development of these programs. CMS crisis response support also includes crisis stabilization centers, which Beronio noted may help reduce emergency room volumes and arrests. In closing, she stated that CMS will host a webinar series addressing maternal mental health and substance use.

Improving the Provision of Care: Beyond Screening

Gathing began with an overview of Humana Incorporated, noting that it is relatively new in Medicaid. She described the benefits of various mental health services and noted that individuals should have a personalized assessment to determine the care needed. Additional complexity occurs when integrating outside care providers, such as community health workers or doulas, into the care team, Gathing aid.

Gathing described managed care and the importance of considering whether patients are served in the most effective ways and identifying inefficiencies in the system. She said that the best way to move beyond screening is education, raising awareness, and building and bolstering infrastructure. She added that Humana has been assisting states with accessing grant funding to set up EHRs to improve mental health services integration. Because of clinician shortages, Gathing said screening is counterproductive without workforce expansion. She suggested leveraging community care to expand access and reduce costs. She also noted updates and improvements to billing and payment processes and discussed alternative payment models, which shift payment from being "volume driven" to "value oriented," aligning reimbursement with cost-efficient, high-quality care. She said that population-based payments tied to performance enable greater flexibility in service delivery and provide a more meaningful financial incentive than fee-for-service models. She explained that value-based payment models compensate health care providers for improving health outcomes and meeting quality measures. They can be designed to cover a range of services or focus on specific populations and may help to integrate mental and behavioral health into primary care.

Gathing highlighted the CMS Innovation in Behavioral Health Model, which aims to bridge the gap between behavioral and physical health within a community-based behavioral health practice. This program, launched in January 2024, is focused on improving the quality of care provided and behavioral and physical health outcomes for Medicaid and Medicare populations with moderate to severe mental health conditions and SUD. Gathing added that these patients face disproportionately higher rates of mental health conditions and SUD and so are more likely to experience poor physical health outcomes, frequent visits to the emergency room, and premature death. Gathing reiterated the importance of screening for SDOH to identify and address barriers to care for specific patients, which can improve their health outcomes.

Overall, Gathing stated that the health care system suffers from a lack of integration, which slows implementation and impedes access to services and patient care. She noted the importance of developing innovative billing and payment models to cover an expanded health care workforce, including care providers such as doulas.

Gathing suggested using universal language to discuss patient needs, risk, and severity. She also suggested an increased focus on women in a transition period, such as the transition to motherhood, when it may be hardest for them to follow up with referrals. Adopting universal EHRs would improve this process, she said. In closing, Gathing reiterated the many benefits of an integrated, collaborative care model.

Discussion

Fields Allsbrook asked how CMS tracks or monitors reimbursement rates around managed care. Beronio said additional guidance will be released summer 2024 and that CMS is focused on improving monitoring and reporting by states. Lewis Johnson said the presentations highlighted that women with the most needs are not getting necessary care and asked the presenters for ideas to improve care access across the life-span for those at the highest risk for poor mental health outcomes. Beronio suggested increased integration of mental health care into mainstream care settings, including team-based approaches in primary care offices. She noted that this could allow health care providers to "meet women where they are" and enable practices to hire additional nurses and case managers. She also suggested expanding and better implementing crisis support services, such as hotlines. Beronio noted that the Certified Community Behavioral Health Clinical Demonstration, in partnership with SAMHSA, is providing increases in federal reimbursements for states working to offer comprehensive, community-based services. Gathing emphasized the importance of a network or directory of mental health care providers who can connect and collaborate. Screening is the first step, she said, but without improvements to infrastructure, referrals, and follow-up may not occur.

Nelson commented on Gathing's suggestion for using colocation to improve access to a wider variety of providers. She said that this model was incorporated in her clinical practice and both speeds the referral process and improves collaborative care.

Monk asked about parity laws, stating her fear that top health care providers will stop accepting public insurance, due to low payment. Beronio replied that the problem is due to both low reimbursement amounts and the administrative burden of filing claims. She noted that workforce shortages exacerbate these challenges.

Sheth closed by noting the interconnectedness of women's mental health care and other larger sociopolitical issues, such as income gaps and other labor issues. She called for leaders in health care to become more involved with this broader set of intersecting issues, recognizing that many seemingly disparate challenges impact patients' lives at a community level.

CLOSING REMARKS

Closing remarks were delivered by Vivian W. Pinn, retired from the Office of Research on Women's Health at NIH. Pinn highlighted repeated themes learned throughout the workshop, such as the need for improvements to the health care system and the importance of treating the whole person. Key concepts that drive disparities are SDOH and ACEs. Pinn noted that factors that uniquely impact women include excessive caregiving burdens, hormonal shifts across the life-span, stigma and stereotypes, and structural factors that serve as barriers to access, especially in rural areas, for women with disabilities and historically marginalized communities. She reflected on the concept of intersectionality to better address the needs of diverse communities.

Pinn said that a focus on evidence-based approaches and initiatives is important for the future of women's mental health and emphasized the importance of training primary care providers, community health workers, and maternal health care providers to screen for mental health disorders and recognize and address the many overlaps between physical and mental health. Speakers also reviewed the evidence base covering maternal health and how it impacts infant, child, and familial health, along with the data showing the multigenerational impact of maternal and postpartum mental health conditions, including lower scores on cognitive tests for children raised by mothers with depression and the higher risk of suicidal thoughts and behaviors in children with a family history of major depression. She said that preventing maternal mental health conditions can improve the health of multiple generations.

Another point that Pinn highlighted was the repeated calls for improvements to education for clinicians and patients. Education for patients is key for reducing stigma, improving perception of symptoms, and better equipping women and girls to understand and tolerate their symptoms and experiences. Pinn said that additional training for physicians and other health care professionals can better ensure that care needs are met in a wider variety of settings, and she emphasized HRSA's unique role in designing these educational initiatives.

Pinn noted the policy topics that were covered and the need to ensure effective implementation of mental health care policies that improve access for marginalized populations. Pinn echoed the repeated calls for clinicians to collaborate with community care and mental health "extenders." There must be partnership with communities, Pinn said, during both the design and implementation phases of mental health care programs, to adequately address these issues. She also reflected on the many presenters who expressed the need for primary care physicians to be trained in mental health screening, referral, and care. Pinn noted she hoped that the meaningful conversations that began at the workshop would inform the ongoing work of clinicians and researchers.

REFERENCES

Aartsen, M., and M. Jylhä. 2011. Onset of loneliness in older adults: Results of a 28 year prospective study. *European Journal of Ageing* 8(1):31–38.

ACC/AHA (American College of Cardiology/American Heart Association). 2019. Correction to: 2019 ACC/AHA guideline on the primary prevention of cardiovascular disease: Executive summary: A report of the American College of Cardiology/American Heart Association Task Force on Clinical Practice Guidelines. *Circulation* 140(11):e647–e648.

ACOG (American College of Obstetricians and Gynecologists). 2023. Management of premenstrual disorders clinical practice guideline number 7. *The American College of Obstetricians and Gynecologists.*

Admon, L. K., V. K. Dalton, G. E. Kolenic, S. L. Ettner, A. Tilea, R. L. Haffajee, R. M. Brownlee, M. K. Zochowski, K. M. Tabb, M. Muzik, and K. Zivin. 2021. Trends in suicidality 1 year before and after birth among commercially insured childbearing individuals in the United States, 2006–2017. *JAMA Psychiatry* 78(2):171–176.

Aguillard, K., R. B. Hughes, V. R. Schick, S. A. McCurdy, and G. L. Gemeinhardt. 2022. Mental healthcare. *Violence and Victims* 37(1):26–43.

AHRQ (Agency for Healthcare Research and Quality). 2009. Non-pharmacologic interventions for treatment-resistant depression in adults—research protocol document. https://effectivehealthcare.ahrq.gov/products/treatment-resistant-depression/research-protocol (accessed June 12, 2024).

Albert, P. R. 2015. Why is depression more prevalent in women? *Journal of Psychiatry & Neuroscience* 40(4):219–221.

Alegría, M., L. R. Fortuna, J. Y. Lin, F. H. Norris, S. Gao, D. T. Takeuchi, J. S. Jackson, P. E. Shrout, and A. Valentine. 2013. Prevalence, risk, and correlates of posttraumatic stress disorder across ethnic and racial minority groups in the United States. *Medical Care* 51(12):1114–1123.

Almanza, J. I., J. Karbeah, K. M. Tessier, C. Neerland, K. Stoll, R. R. Hardeman, and S. Vedam. 2022. The impact of culturally-centered care on peripartum experiences of autonomy and respect in community birth centers: A comparative study. *Maternal and Child Health Journal* 26(4):895–904.

Altemus, M., N. Sarvaiya, and C. Neill Epperson. 2014. Sex differences in anxiety and depression clinical perspectives. *Frontiers in Neuroendocrinology* 35(3):320–330.

Andreas, S., H. Schulz, J. Volkert, M. Dehoust, S. Sehner, A. Suling, B. Ausín, A. Canuto, M. Crawford, C. Da Ronch, L. Grassi, Y. Hershkovitz, M. Muñoz, A. Quirk, O. Rotenstein, A. B. Santos-Olmo, A. Shalev, J. Strehle, K. Weber, K. Wegscheider, H. U. Wittchen, and M. Härter. 2017. Prevalence of mental disorders in elderly people: The European MentDis_ICF65+ study. *The British Journal of Psychiatry* 210(2):125–131.

Andreescu, C., O. Ajilore, H. J. Aizenstein, K. Albert, M. A. Butters, B. A. Landman, H. T. Karim, R. Krafty, and W. D. Taylor. 2019. Disruption of neural homeostasis as a model of relapse and recurrence in late-life depression. *The American Journal of Geriatric Psychiatry* 27(12):1316–1330.

APA (American Psychological Association). 2013. *Diagnostic and statistical manual of mental disorders: DSM-5.* Vol. 5. Washington, DC: American Psychiatric Association.

APA. 2023. *Health advisory on social media use in adolescence.* Washington, DC: American Psychological Association.

Arnett, D. K., R. S. Blumenthal, M. A. Albert, A. B. Buroker, Z. D. Goldberger, E. J. Hahn, C. D. Himmelfarb, A. Khera, D. Lloyd-Jones, and J. W. McEvoy. 2019. 2019 ACC/AHA guideline on the primary prevention of cardiovascular disease: Executive summary: A report of the American College of Cardiology/American Heart Association Task Force on Clinical Practice Guidelines. *Circulation* 140(11):e563–e595.

Avis, N. E., S. L. Crawford, G. Greendale, J. T. Bromberger, S. A. Everson-Rose, E. B. Gold, R. Hess, H. Joffe, H. M. Kravitz, P. G. Tepper, and R. C. Thurston. 2015. Duration of menopausal vasomotor symptoms over the menopause transition. *JAMA Internal Medicine* 175(4):531–539.

Babineau, V., C. A. McCormack, T. Feng, S. Lee, O. Berry, B. T. Knight, J. D. Newport, Z. N. Stowe, and C. Monk. 2022. Pregnant women with bipolar disorder who have a history of childhood maltreatment: Intergenerational effects of trauma on fetal neurodevelopment and birth outcomes. *Bipolar Disorders* 24(6):671–682.

Bahrami, F., and N. Yousefi. 2011. Females are more anxious than males: A metacognitive perspective. *Iranian Journal of Psychiatry and Behavioral Sciences* 5(2):83–90.

Barger, S. D., N. Messerli-Bürgy, and J. Barth. 2014. Social relationship correlates of major depressive disorder and depressive symptoms in Switzerland: Nationally representative cross sectional study. *BMC Public Health* 14:273.

Barnes, T. L., S. MacLeod, R. Tkatch, M. Ahuja, L. Albright, J. A. Schaeffer, and C. S. Yeh. 2022. Cumulative effect of loneliness and social isolation on health outcomes among older adults. *Aging & Mental Health* 26(7):1327–1334.

Beekman, A. T., E. de Beurs, A. J. van Balkom, D. J. Deeg, R. van Dyck, and W. van Tilburg. 2000. Anxiety and depression in later life: Co-occurrence and communality of risk factors. *The American Journal of Psychiatry* 157(1):89–95.

Belz, F. F., N. J. Vega Potler, I. N. Johnson, and R. P. Wolthusen. 2024. Lessons from low-and middle-income countries: Alleviating the behavioral health workforce shortage in the United States. *Psychiatric Services*: 20230348.

Bergink, V., N. Rasgon, and K. L. Wisner. 2016. Postpartum psychosis: Madness, mania, and melancholia in motherhood. *The American Journal of Psychiatry* 173(12):1179–1188.

Brandon, D. T., L. A. Isaac, and T. A. LaVeist. 2005. The legacy of Tuskegee and trust in medical care: Is Tuskegee responsible for race differences in mistrust of medical care? *JAMA* 97(7):951–956.

Bromberger, J. T., H. M. Kravitz, Y. F. Chang, J. M. Cyranowski, C. Brown, and K. A. Matthews. 2011. Major depression during and after the menopausal transition: Study of women's health across the nation (SWAN). *Psychological Medicine* 41(9):1879-1888.

Brown, C., K. O. Conner, V. C. Copeland, N. Grote, S. Beach, D. Battista, and C. F. Reynolds, III. 2010. Depression stigma, race, and treatment seeking behavior and attitudes. *Journal of Community Psychology* 38(3):350–368.

Brown, L., M. S. Hunter, R. Chen, C. J. Crandall, J. L. Gordon, G. D. Mishra, V. Rother, H. Joffe, and M. Hickey. 2024. Promoting good mental health over the menopause transition. *Lancet* 403(10430):969-983.

Bryant, R. A., L. Kenny, A. Joscelyne, N. Rawson, F. Maccallum, C. Cahill, S. Hopwood, I. Aderka, and A. Nickerson. 2014. Treating prolonged grief disorder: A randomized clinical trial. *JAMA Psychiatry* 71(12):1332–1339.

Bryant, R. A., E. Andrew, and M. S. Korgaonkar. 2021. Distinct neural mechanisms of emotional processing in prolonged grief disorder. *Psychological Medicine* 51(4):587–595.

Bryant-Davis, T., B. Fasalojo, A. Arounian, K. L. Jackson, and E. Leithman. 2024. Resist and rise: A trauma-informed womanist model for group therapy. *Women & Therapy* 47(1):34–57.

Burholt, V., and T. Scharf. 2014. Poor health and loneliness in later life: The role of depressive symptoms, social resources, and rural environments. *The Journals of Gerontology, Series B* 69(2):311–324.

Burnett-Zeigler, I., S. Schuette, D. Victorson, and K. L. Wisner. 2016. Mind-body approaches to treating mental health symptoms among disadvantaged populations: A comprehensive review. *Journal of Alternative and Complementary Medicine* 22(2):115–124.

CAP (Center for American Progress). 2015. *A fair shot for workers with disabilities.* Center for American Progress.

Carmona, S., M. Martínez-García, M. Paternina-Die, E. Barba-Müller, L. M. Wierenga, Y. Alemán-Gómez, C. Pretus, L. Marcos-Vidal, L. Beumala, R. Cortizo, C. Pozzobon, M. Picado, F. Lucco, D. García-García, J. C. Soliva, A. Tobeña, J. S. Peper, E. A. Crone, A. Ballesteros, O. Vilarroya, M. Desco, and E. Hoekzema. 2019. Pregnancy and adolescence entail similar neuroanatomical adaptations: A comparative analysis of cerebral morphometric changes. *Human Brain Mapping* 40(7):2143–2152.

Carter, E. B., L. A. Temming, J. Akin, S. Fowler, G. A. Macones, G. A. Colditz, and M. G. Tuuli. 2016. Group prenatal care compared with traditional prenatal care: A systematic review and meta-analysis. *Obstetrics & Gynecology* 128(3):551–561.

CDC (Centers for Disease Control and Prevention). 2017. *Table 15. Life expectancy at birth, at age 65, and at age 75, by sex, race, and Hispanic origin: United States, selected years 1900–2016.* https://www.cdc.gov/nchs/data/hus/2017/015.pdf (accessed June 18, 2024).

CDC. 2023. *Anxiety and depression in children: Get the facts.* https://www.cdc.gov/childrensmentalhealth/features/anxiety-depression-children.html (accessed June 14, 2024).

Center on the Developing Child. 2009. *Maternal depression can undermine the development of young children.* Cambridge, MA. Harvard University.

Chiaramonte, D., M. Ring, and A. B. Locke. 2017. Integrative women's health. *Medical Clinics of North America* 101(5):955–975.

Chin, J. L., B. W. Yee, and M. E. Banks. 2014. Women's health and behavioral health issues in health care reform. *Journal of Social Work in Disability & Rehabilitation* 13(1–2):122–138.

CMS (Centers for Medicare & Medicaid Services). 2023. *Request for comments on processes for assessing compliance with mental health parity and addiction equity in Medicaid and CHIP.* https://www.medicaid.gov/sites/default/files/2023–09/cmcs-mental-health-parity-092023.pdf (accessed June 14, 2024).

Compton, S. N., J. T. Walkup, A. M. Albano, J. C. Piacentini, B. Birmaher, J. T. Sherrill, G. S. Ginsburg, M. A. Rynn, J. T. McCracken, B. D. Waslick, S. Iyengar, P. C. Kendall, and J. S. March. 2010. Child/adolescent anxiety multimodal study (CAMS): Rationale, design, and methods. *Child and Adolescent Psychiatry and Mental Health* 4:1.

Conner, K. O., B. Lee, V. Mayers, D. Robinson, C. F. Reynolds III, S. Albert, and C. Brown. 2010. Attitudes and beliefs about mental health among African American older adults suffering from depression. *Journal of Aging Studies* 24(4):266–277.

Cook, N., S. Ayers, and A. Horsch. 2018. Maternal posttraumatic stress disorder during the perinatal period and child outcomes: A systematic review. *Journal of Affective Disorders* 225:18–31.

Cudjoe, T. K. M., D. L. Roth, S. L. Szanton, J. L. Wolff, C. M. Boyd, and R. J. Thorpe. 2020. The epidemiology of social isolation: National Health and Aging Trends study. *The Journals of Gerontology, Series B* 75(1):107–113.

Deligiannidis, K. M., S. Meltzer-Brody, H. Gunduz-Bruce, J. Doherty, J. Jonas, S. Li, A. J. Sankoh, C. Silber, A. D. Campbell, and B. Werneburg. 2021. Effect of zuranolone vs. placebo in postpartum depression: A randomized clinical trial. *JAMA Psychiatry* 78(9):951–959.

Di Benedetto, M. G., P. Landi, C. Mencacci, and A. Cattaneo. 2024. Depression in women: Potential biological and sociocultural factors driving the sex effect. *Neuropsychobiology* 83(1):2–16.

Dias, R. S., F. Kerr-Corrêa, R. A. Moreno, L. A. Trinca, A. Pontes, H. W. Halbe, A. Gianfaldoni, and I. S. Dalben. 2006. Efficacy of hormone therapy with and without methyltestosterone augmentation of venlafaxine in the treatment of postmenopausal depression: A double-blind controlled pilot study. *Menopause* 13(2):202–211.

Domènech-Abella, J., E. Lara, M. Rubio-Valera, B. Olaya, M. V. Moneta, L. A. Rico-Uribe, J. L. Ayuso-Mateos, J. Mundó, and J. M. Haro. 2017. Loneliness and depression in the elderly: The role of social network. *Social Psychiatry and Psychiatric Epidemiology* 52(4):381–390.

Donnelly, R., H. Cha, and D. Umberson. 2022. Multiple family member deaths and cardiometabolic health among Black and White older adults. *Journal of Health and Social Behavior* 63(4):610–625.

Donovan, N. J., J. J. Locascio, G. A. Marshall, J. Gatchel, B. J. Hanseeuw, D. M. Rentz, K. A. Johnson, and R. A. Sperling. 2018. Longitudinal association of amyloid beta and anxious-depressive symptoms in cognitively normal older adults. *The American Journal of Psychiatry* 175(6):530–537.

Dunn, D. S. 2019. Outsider privileges can lead to insider disadvantages: Some psychosocial aspects of ableism. *Journal of Social Issues* 75(3):665–682.

Dykstra, P. A., T. G. Van Tilburg, and J. D. J. Gierveld. 2005. Changes in older adult loneliness: Results from a seven-year longitudinal study. *Research on Aging* 27(6):725–747.

Eisenlohr-Moul, T., M. Divine, K. Schmalenberger, L. Murphy, B. Buchert, M. Wagner-Schuman, A. Kania, S. Raja, A. B. Miller, J. Barone, and J. Ross. 2022. Prevalence of lifetime self-injurious thoughts and behaviors in a global sample of 599 patients reporting prospectively confirmed diagnosis with premenstrual dysphoric disorder. *BMC Psychiatry* 22(1):199.

Epperson, C. N., M. Steiner, S. A. Hartlage, E. Eriksson, P. J. Schmidt, I. Jones, and K. A. Yonkers. 2012. Premenstrual dysphoric disorder: Evidence for a new category for DSM-5. *The American Journal of Psychiatry* 169(5):465–475.

Eyre, H. A., L. E. Stirland, D. V. Jeste, C. F. Reynolds, III, M. Berk, A. Ibanez, W. D. Dawson, B. Lawlor, I. Leroi, and K. Yaffe. 2023. Life-course brain health as a determinant of late-life mental health: American Association for Geriatric Psychiatry expert panel recommendations. *The American Journal of Geriatric Psychiatry* 31(12):1017–1031.

Faubion, S. S., F. Enders, M. S. Hedges, R. Chaudhry, J. M. Kling, C. L. Shufelt, M. Saadedine, K. Mara, J. M. Griffin, and E. Kapoor. 2023. Impact of menopause symptoms on women in the workplace. Paper read at Mayo Clinic Proceedings.

Fisher, C. L., K. B. Wright, C. J. Rising, X. Cai, M. D. Mullis, A. Burke-Garcia, and D. Afanaseva. 2020. Helping mothers and daughters talk about environmental breast cancer risk and risk-reducing lifestyle behaviors. *International Journal of Environmental Research and Public Health* 17(13).

Forlani, M., M. Morri, M. Belvederi Murri, V. Bernabei, F. Moretti, T. Attili, A. Biondini, D. De Ronchi, and A. R. Atti. 2014. Anxiety symptoms in 74+ community-dwelling elderly: Associations with physical morbidity, depression and alcohol consumption. *PLoS One* 9(2):e89859.

Freeman, E. W., M. D. Sammel, and R. J. Sanders. 2014. Risk of long-term hot flashes after natural menopause: Evidence from the Penn Ovarian Aging Study cohort. *Menopause* 21(9):924–932.

Gartoulla, P., R. Worsley, R. J. Bell, and S. R. Davis. 2015. Moderate to severe vasomotor and sexual symptoms remain problematic for women aged 60 to 65 years. *Menopause* 22(7):694–701.

Gehlert, S., I. H. Song, C. H. Chang, and S. A. Hartlage. 2009. The prevalence of premenstrual dysphoric disorder in a randomly selected group of urban and rural women. *Psychological Medicine* 39(1):129–136.

Geronimus, A. T., M. Hicken, D. Keene, and J. Bound. 2006. "Weathering" and age patterns of allostatic load scores among Blacks and Whites in the United States. *American Journal of Public Health* 96(5):826–833.

Ginsburg, G. S., E. M. Becker-Haimes, C. Keeton, P. C. Kendall, S. Iyengar, D. Sakolsky, A. M. Albano, T. Peris, S. N. Compton, and J. Piacentini. 2018. Results from the child/adolescent anxiety multimodal extended long-term study (CAMELS): Primary anxiety outcomes. *Journal of the American Academy of Child and Adolescent Psychiatry* 57(7):471–480.

Gleason, C. E., N. M. Dowling, W. Wharton, J. E. Manson, V. M. Miller, C. S. Atwood, E. A. Brinton, M. I. Cedars, R. A. Lobo, G. R. Merriam, G. Neal-Perry, N. F. Santoro, H. S. Taylor, D. M. Black, M. J. Budoff, H. N. Hodis, F. Naftolin, S. M. Harman, and S. Asthana. 2015. Effects of hormone therapy on cognition and mood in recently postmenopausal women: Findings from the randomized, controlled KEEPS-cognitive and affective study. *PLOS Medicine* 12(6):e1001833; discussion e1001833.

Gold, E. B., A. Colvin, N. Avis, J. Bromberger, G. A. Greendale, L. Powell, B. Sternfeld, and K. Matthews. 2006. Longitudinal analysis of the association between vasomotor symptoms and race/ethnicity across the menopausal transition: Study of Women's Health Across the Nation. *American Journal of Public Health* 96(7):1226–1235.

Golden, J., R. M. Conroy, I. Bruce, A. Denihan, E. Greene, M. Kirby, and B. A. Lawlor. 2011. The spectrum of worry in the community-dwelling elderly. *Aging & Mental Health* 15(8):985–994.

Gordon, J. L., D. R. Rubinow, T. A. Eisenlohr-Moul, K. Xia, P. J. Schmidt, and S. S. Girdler. 2018. Efficacy of transdermal estradiol and micronized progesterone in the prevention of depressive symptoms in the menopause transition: A randomized clinical trial. *JAMA Psychiatry* 75(2):149–157.

Greenman, E., and Y. Xie. 2008. Double jeopardy? The interaction of gender and race on earnings in the United States. *Social Forces* 86(3):1217–1244.

Grote, N. K., S. E. Bledsoe, J. Wellman, and C. Brown. 2007. Depression in African American and White women with low incomes: The role of chronic stress. *Social Work in Public Health* 23(2–3):59–88.

Gwynn, R. C., H. L. McQuistion, K. H. McVeigh, R. K. Garg, T. R. Frieden, and L. E. Thorpe. 2008. Prevalence, diagnosis, and treatment of depression and generalized anxiety disorder in a diverse urban community. *Psychiatric Services* 59(6):641–647.

Haight, S. C., J. R. Daw, C. L. Martin, K. Sheffield-Abdullah, S. Verbiest, B. W. Pence, and J. Maselko. 2024. Racial and ethnic inequities in postpartum depressive symptoms, diagnosis, and care in 7 U.S. jurisdictions: Study examines racial and ethnic inequities in postpartum depressive symptoms, diagnosis, and care. *Health Affairs* 43(4):486–495.

Halbreich, U., J. Borenstein, T. Pearlstein, and L. S. Kahn. 2003. The prevalence, impairment, impact, and burden of premenstrual dysphoric disorder (PMS/PMDD). *Psychoneuroendocrinology* 28 Suppl 3:1–23.

Harlow, S. D., S. M. Burnett-Bowie, G. A. Greendale, N. E. Avis, A. N. Reeves, T. R. Richards, and T. T. Lewis. 2022. Disparities in reproductive aging and midlife health between Black and White women: The study of Women's Health Across the Nation (SWAN). *Women's Midlife Health* 8(1):3.

Hartlage, S. A., D. L. Brandenburg, and H. M. Kravitz. 2004. Premenstrual exacerbation of depressive disorders in a community-based sample in the United States. *Psychosomatic Medicine* 66(5):698–706.

Hasin, D. S., R. D. Goodwin, F. S. Stinson, and B. F. Grant. 2005. Epidemiology of major depressive disorder: Results from the National Epidemiologic Survey on Alcoholism and Related Conditions. *Archives of General Psychiatry* 62(10):1097–1106.

Hawkley, L. C., S. Buecker, T. Kaiser, and M. Luhmann. 2022. Loneliness from young adulthood to old age: Explaining age differences in loneliness. *International Journal of Behavioral Development* 46(1):39–49.

Hernandez, N. D., S. Francis, M. Allen, E. Bellamy, O. T. Sims, H. Oh, D. Guillaume, A. Parker, and R. Chandler. 2022. Prevalence and predictors of symptoms of perinatal mood and anxiety disorders among a sample of urban Black women in the South. *Maternal and Child Health Journal* 26(4):770–777.

Hill, S. E., and S. Mengelkoch. 2023. Moving beyond the mean: Promising research pathways to support a precision medicine approach to hormonal contraception. *Frontiers in Neuroendocrinology* 68:101042.

Howard, L. M., and H. Khalifeh. 2020. Perinatal mental health: A review of progress and challenges. *World Psychiatry* 19(3):313–327.

Hughes, M. E., L. J. Waite, L. C. Hawkley, and J. T. Cacioppo. 2004. A short scale for measuring loneliness in large surveys: Results from two population-based studies. *Research on Aging* 26(6):655–672.

Hylan, T. R., K. Sundell, and R. Judge. 1999. The impact of premenstrual symptomatology on functioning and treatment-seeking behavior: Experience from the United States, United Kingdom, and France. *Journal of Women's Health & Gender-Based Medicine* 8(8):1043–1052.

Ickovics, J. R., T. S. Kershaw, C. Westdahl, U. Magriples, Z. Massey, H. Reynolds, and S. S. Rising. 2007. Group prenatal care and perinatal outcomes: A randomized controlled trial. *Obstetrics & Gynecology* 110(2 Part 1):330–339.

IOM (Institute of Medicine). 2011. *Clinical preventative services for women: Closing the gaps.* Washington, DC: National Academies Press.

Joffe, H., H. Groninger, C. Soares, R. Nonacs, and L. S. Cohen. 2001. An open trial of mirtazapine in menopausal women with depression unresponsive to estrogen replacement therapy. *Journal of Women's Health & Gender-Based Medicine* 10(10):999–1004.

Joffe, H., L. F. Petrillo, A. C. Viguera, H. Gottshcall, C. N. Soares, J. E. Hall, and L. S. Cohen. 2007. Treatment of premenstrual worsening of depression with adjunctive oral contraceptive pills: A preliminary report. *The Journal of Clinical Psychiatry* 68(12):1954–1962.

Joffe, H., A. de Wit, J. Coborn, S. Crawford, M. Freeman, A. Wiley, G. Athappilly, S. Kim, K. A. Sullivan, L. S. Cohen, and J. E. Hall. 2019. Impact of estradiol variability and progesterone on mood in perimenopausal women with depressive symptoms. *The Journal of Clinical Endocrinology & Metabolism* 105(3):e642–e650.

Johnson, A., L. Roberts, and G. Elkins. 2019. Complementary and alternative medicine for menopause. *Journal of Evidence-Based Integrative Medicine* 24:2515690X19829380.

Jones, H. J., M. Butsch Kovacic, J. Lambert, W. a. R. Almallah, R. Becker, L. de Las Fuentes, and T. Bakas. 2022. A randomized feasibility trial of the midlife Black women's stress and wellness intervention (B-SWELL); a community participatory intervention to increase adoption of life's simple 7 healthy lifestyle behaviors. *Translational Behavioral Medicine* 12(11):1084–1095.

Kannan, V. D., and P. J. Veazie. 2023. U.S. trends in social isolation, social engagement, and companionship—nationally and by age, sex, race/ethnicity, family income, and work hours, 2003–2020. *Social Science & Medicine—Population Health* 21:101331.

Karim, H. T., S. Lee, A. Gerlach, M. Stinley, R. Berta, R. Mahbubani, D. L. Tudorascu, M. A. Butters, J. J. Gross, and C. Andreescu. 2024. Hippocampal subfield volume in older adults with and without mild cognitive impairment: Effects of worry and cognitive reappraisal. *Neurobiology of Aging.*

Karim, H. T., M. Ly, G. Yu, R. Krafty, D. L. Tudorascu, H. J. Aizenstein, and C. Andreescu. 2021. Aging faster: Worry and rumination in late life are associated with greater brain age. *Neurobiology of Aging* 101:13–21.

Karim, H. T., C. Andreescu, D. Tudorascu, S. F. Smagula, M. A. Butters, J. F. Karp, C. Reynolds, and H. J. Aizenstein. 2017. Intrinsic functional connectivity in late-life depression: Trajectories over the course of pharmacotherapy in remitters and non-remitters. *Molecular Psychiatry* 22(3):450–457.

Kertz, S. J., J. S. Bigda-Peyton, D. H. Rosmarin, and T. Björgvinsson. 2012. The importance of worry across diagnostic presentations: Prevalence, severity and associated symptoms in a partial hospital setting. *Journal of Anxiety Disorders* 26(1):126–133.

Kessler, R. C., P. Berglund, O. Demler, R. Jin, D. Koretz, K. R. Merikangas, A. J. Rush, E. E. Walters, and P. S. Wang. 2003. The epidemiology of major depressive disorder: Results from the national Comorbidity Survey Replication (NCS-R). *JAMA* 289(23):3095–3105.

Kiesner, J., T. A. Eisenlohr-Moul, and G. Vidotto. 2022. Affective risk associated with menstrual cycle symptom change. *Frontiers in Global Women's Health* 3:896924.

Kilpatrick, L. A., P. Siddarth, M. M. Milillo, B. Krause-Sorio, L. Ercoli, K. L. Narr, and H. Lavretsky. 2022. Impact of tai chi as an adjunct treatment on brain connectivity in geriatric depression. *Journal of Affective Disorders* 315:1–6.

Kobylski, L. A., J. Keller, S. D. Molock, and H.-N. Le. 2023. Preventing perinatal suicide: An unmet public health need. *The Lancet Public Health* 8(6):e402.

Kornstein, S. G., Q. Jiang, S. Reddy, J. J. Musgnung, and C. J. Guico-Pabia. 2010. Short-term efficacy and safety of desvenlafaxine in a randomized, placebo-controlled study of perimenopausal and postmenopausal women with major depressive disorder. *The Journal of Clinical Psychiatry* 71(8):1088–1096.

Kornstein, S. G., A. Clayton, W. Bao, and C. J. Guico-Pabia. 2014a. Post hoc analysis of the efficacy and safety of desvenlafaxine 50 mg/day in a randomized, placebo-controlled study of perimenopausal and postmenopausal women with major depressive disorder. *Menopause* 21(8):799–806.

Kornstein, S. G., R. D. Pedersen, P. J. Holland, C. B. Nemeroff, A. J. Rothschild, M. E. Thase, M. H. Trivedi, P. T. Ninan, and M. B. Keller. 2014b. Influence of sex and menopausal status on response, remission, and recurrence in patients with recurrent major depressive disorder treated with venlafaxine extended release or fluoxetine: Analysis of data from the prevent study. *The Journal of Clinical Psychiatry* 75(1):62–68.

Kotwal, A. A., I. S. Cenzer, L. J. Waite, K. E. Covinsky, C. M. Perissinotto, W. J. Boscardin, L. C. Hawkley, W. Dale, and A. K. Smith. 2021. The epidemiology of social isolation and loneliness among older adults during the last years of life. *Journal of the American Geriatrics Society* 69(11):3081–3091.

Kravitz, H. M., I. Janssen, J. T. Bromberger, K. A. Matthews, M. H. Hall, K. Ruppert, and H. Joffe. 2017. Sleep trajectories before and after the final menstrual period in the study of women's health across the nation (swan). *Current Sleep Medicine Reports* 3(3):235–250.

Kumar, R. M. 2023. The many faces of grief: A systematic literature review of grief during the COVID-19 pandemic. *Illness, Crisis & Loss* 31(1):100–119.

Lavretsky, H., P. Siddarth, V. Kepe, L. M. Ercoli, K. J. Miller, A. C. Burggren, S. Y. Bookheimer, S.-C. Huang, J. R. Barrio, and G. W. Small. 2009. Depression and anxiety symptoms are associated with cerebral fddnp-pet binding in middle-aged and older nondemented adults. *The American Journal of Geriatric Psychiatry* 17(6):493–502.

Leath, S., M. K. Jones, and S. Butler-Barnes. 2022. An examination of ACEs, the internalization of the superwoman schema, and mental health outcomes among Black adult women. *Journal of Trauma & Dissociation* 23(3):307–323.

Lee, D. Y., C. Andreescu, H. Aizenstein, H. Karim, A. Mizuno, A. Kolobaric, S. Yoon, Y. Kim, J. Lim, E. J. Hwang, Y. T. Ouh, H. H. Kim, S. J. Son, and R. W. Park. 2023. Impact of symptomatic menopausal transition on the occurrence of depression, anxiety, and sleep disorders: A real-world multi-site study. *European Psychiatry* 66(1):e80.

Lenger, M. K., M. A. Neergaard, M.-B. Guldin, and M. K. Nielsen. 2020. Poor physical and mental health predicts prolonged grief disorder: A prospective, population-based cohort study on caregivers of patients at the end of life. *Palliative Medicine* 34(10):1416–1424.

Lenze, S. N., K. McKay-Gist, R. Paul, M. Tepe, K. Mathews, S. Kornfield, C. Phillips, R. Smith, A. Stoermer, and E. B. Carter. 2024. Elevating voices, addressing depression, toxic stress, and equity through group prenatal care: A pilot study. *Health Equity* 8(1):87–95.

Lewis, K. C., M. J. Roche, F. Brown, and J. G. Tillman. 2023. Attachment, loneliness, and social connection as prospective predictors of suicidal ideation during the COVID-19 pandemic: A relational diathesis-stress experience sampling study. *Suicide and Life-Threatening Behavior* 53(1):64–74.

Lewis, T. T., M. E. Van Dyke, K. A. Matthews, and E. Barinas-Mitchell. 2021. Race/ethnicity, cumulative midlife loss, and carotid atherosclerosis in middle-aged women. *American Journal of Epidemiology* 190(4):576–587.

Maki, P. M., S. G. Kornstein, H. Joffe, J. T. Bromberger, E. W. Freeman, G. Athappilly, W. V. Bobo, L. H. Rubin, H. K. Koleva, L. S. Cohen, and C. N. Soares. 2019. Guidelines for the evaluation and treatment of perimenopausal depression: Summary and recommendations. *Journal of Women's Health (Larchmont)* 28(2):117-134.

Manning, R. B., III, R. Cipollina, S. R. Lowe, K. R. Bogart, J. M. Ostrove, J. M. Adler, M. R. Nario-Redmond, and K. Wang. 2023. Barriers to mental health service use among people with disabilities during the COVID-19 pandemic. *Rehabilitation Psychology* 68(4): 351 – 361.

McEvoy, K., and L. M. Osborne. 2019. Allopregnanolone and reproductive psychiatry: An overview. *International Review of Psychiatry* 31(3):237–244.

Mengelkoch, S., and G. M. Slavich. 2024. Sex differences in stress susceptibility as a key mechanism underlying depression risk. *Current Psychiatry Reports* 26(4):157–165.

Mengelkoch, S., J. Gassen, G. M. Slavich, and S. E. Hill. 2024. Hormonal contraceptive use is associated with differences in women's inflammatory and psychological reactivity to an acute social stressor. *Brain, Behavior, and Immunity* 115:747–757.

MHA (Mental Health America). n.d. *Native and indigenous communities and mental health.* https://www.mhanational.org/issues/native-and-indigenous-communities-and-mental-health (accessed June 14, 2024).

Mogensen, L., and W. Hu. 2019. "A doctor who really knows…": A survey of community perspectives on medical students and practitioners with disability. *BMC Medical Education* 19:1–10.

Morrison, M. F., M. J. Kallan, T. Ten Have, I. Katz, K. Tweedy, and M. Battistini. 2004. Lack of efficacy of estradiol for depression in postmenopausal women: A randomized, controlled trial. *Biological Psychiatry* 55(4):406–412.

Mukherjee, S., D. R. Velez Edwards, D. D. Baird, D. A. Savitz, and K. E. Hartmann. 2013. Risk of miscarriage among Black women and White women in a U.S. prospective cohort study. *American Journal of Epidemiology* 177(11):1271–1278.

NASEM (National Academies of Sciences, Engineering, and Medicine). 2020. *Social isolation and loneliness in older adults: Opportunities for the health care system.* Washington, DC: The National Academies Press.

NASEM. 2023. *Achieving whole health: A new approach for veterans and the nation.* Edited by A. H. Krist, J. South-Paul, and M. Meisnere. Washington, DC: The National Academies Press.

Neal-Barnett, A., R. Stadulis, M. Murray, M. R. Payne, A. Thomas, and B. B. Salley. 2011. Sister circles as a culturally relevant intervention for anxious African American women. *The Clinical Psychologist* 18(3):266–273.

Newall, N. E., J. G. Chipperfield, and D. S. Bailis. 2014. Predicting stability and change in loneliness in later life. *Journal of Social and Personal Relationships* 31(3):335–351.

Nicolaisen, M., and K. Thorsen. 2014. Who are lonely? Loneliness in different age groups (18–81 years old), using two measures of loneliness. *The International Journal of Aging and Human Development* 78(3):229–257.

NIH (National Institutes of Health). 2005. National Institutes of Health State of the Science Conference statement on manifestations and management of chronic insomnia in adults, June 13–15, 2005. *Sleep* 28(9):1049–1057.

Njoku, A., M. Evans, L. Nimo-Sefah, and J. Bailey. 2023. Listen to the whispers before they become screams: Addressing Black maternal morbidity and mortality in the United States. Paper read at Healthcare.

Nnoli, A. 2023. Historical primer on obstetrics and gynecology health inequities in America: A narrative review of four events. *Obstetrics and Gynecology* 142(4):779–786.

Nolan, L. N., and L. Hughes. 2022. Premenstrual exacerbation of mental health disorders: A systematic review of prospective studies. *Archives of Women's Mental Health* 25(5):831–852.

O'Connor, M.-F., D. K. Wellisch, A. L. Stanton, N. I. Eisenberger, M. R. Irwin, and M. D. Lieberman. 2008. Craving love? Enduring grief activates brain's reward center. *NeuroImage* 42(2):969–972.

Peerenboom, L., R. Collard, P. Naarding, and H. Comijs. 2015. The association between depression and emotional and social loneliness in older persons and the influence of social support, cognitive functioning and personality: A cross-sectional study. *Journal of Affective Disorders* 182:26–31.

Perissinotto, C. M., I. Stijacic Cenzer, and K. E. Covinsky. 2012. Loneliness in older persons: A predictor of functional decline and death. *Archives of Internal Medicine* 172(14):1078–1083.

Petersen, E. E. 2019. Racial/ethnic disparities in pregnancy-related deaths—United States, 2007–2016. *Morbidity and Mortlity Weekly Report* 68.

Pietrzak, R. H., R. B. Goldstein, S. M. Southwick, and B. F. Grant. 2012. Psychiatric comorbidity of full and partial posttraumatic stress disorder among older adults in the United States: Results from Wave 2 of the National Epidemiologic Survey on Alcohol and Related Conditions. *The American Journal of Geriatric Psychiatry* 20(5):380–390.

Pietrzak, R. H., J. C. Scott, A. Neumeister, Y. Y. Lim, D. Ames, K. A. Ellis, K. Harrington, N. T. Lautenschlager, C. Szoeke, and R. N. Martins. 2014. Anxiety symptoms, cerebral amyloid burden and memory decline in healthy older adults without dementia: 3-year prospective cohort study. *The British Journal of Psychiatry* 204(5):400–401.

Pinquart, M., and S. Sörensen. 2006. Gender differences in caregiver stressors, social resources, and health: An updated meta-analysis. *The Journals of Gerontology, Series B* 61(1):P33–45.

Platt, J., S. Prins, L. Bates, and K. Keyes. 2016. Unequal depression for equal work? How the wage gap explains gendered disparities in mood disorders. *Social Science & Medicine* 149:1–8.

Policy Center for Maternal Mental Health. 2023. *American Indian and Alaskan Native maternal mental health.* https://www.issuelab.org/resources/41928/41928.pdf (accessed June 14, 2024).

Randolph, J. F., Jr., H. Zheng, M. R. Sowers, C. Crandall, S. Crawford, E. B. Gold, and M. Vuga. 2011. Change in follicle-stimulating hormone and estradiol across the menopausal transition: Effect of age at the final menstrual period. *Journal of Clinical Endocrinology and Metabolism* 96(3):746–754.

Rapkin, A. J., and E. I. Lewis. 2013. Treatment of premenstrual dysphoric disorder. *Women's Health* 9(6):537–556.

Robertson, E., S. Grace, T. Wallington, and D. E. Stewart. 2004. Antenatal risk factors for postpartum depression: A synthesis of recent literature. *General Hospital Psychiatry* 26(4):289–295.

Ross, J. M., J. C. Barone, H. Tauseef, K. M. Schmalenberger, A. Nagpal, N. A. Crane, and T. A. Eisenlohr-Moul. 2024. Predicting acute changes in suicidal ideation and planning: A longitudinal study of symptom mediators and the role of the menstrual cycle in female psychiatric outpatients with suicidality. *The American Journal of Psychiatry* 181(1):57–67.

Rusch, L. C., J. W. Kanter, R. C. Manos, and C. E. Weeks. 2008. Depression stigma in a predominantly low income African American sample with elevated depressive symptoms. *The Journal of Nervous and Mental Disease* 196(12):919–922.

Saadedine, M. 2023. Caregiving burden linked to more menopause symptoms: Presented at: Annual Meeting of The Menopause Society.

SAMHSA (Substance Abuse and Mental Health Services Administration). 2022. *Highlights for the 2022 National Survey on Drug Use and Health.* https://www.samhsa.gov/data/sites/default/files/reports/rpt42731/2022-nsduh-main-highlights.pdf (accessed June 17, 2024).

SAMHSA. 2023. *Practical guide for implementing a trauma-informed approach.* Washington, DC: Substance Abuse and Mental Health Services Administration.

Santabarbara, J., D. M. Lipnicki, B. Olaya, B. Villagrasa, P. Gracia-Garcia, J. Bueno-Notivol, A. Lobo, and R. Lopez-Anton. 2020. Association between anxiety and vascular dementia risk: New evidence and an updated meta-analysis. *Journal of Clinical Medicine* 9(5):1368.

Saunders, K. E., and K. Hawton. 2006. Suicidal behaviour and the menstrual cycle. *Psychological Medicine* 36(7):901–912.

Schiller, C. E., S. L. Johnson, A. C. Abate, P. J. Schmidt, and D. R. Rubinow. 2016. Reproductive steroid regulation of mood and behavior. *Comprehensive Physiology* 6(3):1135–1160.

Schmalenberger, K. M., T. A. Eisenlohr-Moul, P. Surana, D. R. Rubinow, and S. S. Girdler. 2017. Predictors of premenstrual impairment among women undergoing prospective assessment for premenstrual dysphoric disorder: A cycle-level analysis. *Psychological Medicine* 47(9):1585–1596.

Schmidt, P. J., L. Nieman, M. A. Danaceau, M. B. Tobin, C. A. Roca, J. H. Murphy, and D. R. Rubinow. 2000. Estrogen replacement in perimenopause-related depression: A preliminary report. *American Journal of Obstetrics and Gynecology* 183(2):414–420.

Schweizer-Schubert, S., J. L. Gordon, T. A. Eisenlohr-Moul, S. Meltzer-Brody, K. M. Schmalenberger, R. Slopien, A. L. Zietlow, U. Ehlert, and B. Ditzen. 2020. Steroid hormone sensitivity in reproductive mood disorders: On the role of the gaba(a) receptor complex and stress during hormonal transitions. *Frontiers in Medicine* 7:479646.

Servin-Barthet, C., M. Martínez-García, C. Pretus, M. Paternina-Die, A. Soler, O. Khymenets, J. Pozo Ó, B. Leuner, O. Vilarroya, and S. Carmona. 2023. The transition to motherhood: Linking hormones, brain and behaviour. *Nature reviews. Neuroscience* 24(10):605–619.

Shear, K., E. Frank, P. R. Houck, and C. F. Reynolds, III. 2005. Treatment of complicated grief: A randomized controlled trial. *JAMA* 293(21):2601–2608.

Shear, M. K., Y. Wang, N. Skritskaya, N. Duan, C. Mauro, and A. Ghesquiere. 2014. Treatment of complicated grief in elderly persons: A randomized clinical trial. *JAMA Psychiatry* 71(11):1287–1295.

Shear, M. K., C. F. Reynolds, III, N. M. Simon, S. Zisook, Y. Wang, C. Mauro, N. Duan, B. Lebowitz, and N. Skritskaya. 2016. Optimizing treatment of complicated grief: A randomized clinical trial. *JAMA Psychiatry* 73(7):685–694.

Sibrava, N. J., A. S. Bjornsson, A. C. I. Pérez Benítez, E. Moitra, R. B. Weisberg, and M. B. Keller. 2019. Posttraumatic stress disorder in African American and Latinx adults: Clinical course and the role of racial and ethnic discrimination. *Am Psychol* 74(1):101–116.

Sidebottom, A., M. Vacquier, E. LaRusso, D. Erickson, and R. Hardeman. 2021. Perinatal depression screening practices in a large health system: Identifying current state and assessing opportunities to provide more equitable care. *Archives of Women's Mental Health* 24(1):133–144.

Simon, J. A., R. A. Anderson, E. Ballantyne, J. Bolognese, C. Caetano, H. Joffe, M. Kerr, N. Panay, C. Seitz, and S. Seymore. 2023. Efficacy and safety of elinzanetant, a selective neurokinin-1, 3 receptor antagonist for vasomotor symptoms: A dose-finding clinical trial (SWITCH-1). *Menopause* 30(3):239–246.

Soares, C. N., O. P. Almeida, H. Joffe, and L. S. Cohen. 2001. Efficacy of estradiol for the treatment of depressive disorders in perimenopausal women: A double-blind, randomized, placebo-controlled trial. *Archives of General Psychiatry* 58(6):529–534.

Soares, C. N., J. R. Poitras, J. Prouty, A. B. Alexander, J. L. Shifren, and L. S. Cohen. 2003. Efficacy of citalopram as a monotherapy or as an adjunctive treatment to estrogen therapy for perimenopausal and postmenopausal women with depression and vasomotor symptoms. *The Journal of Clinical Psychiatry* 64(4):473–479.

Strong, K., M. Gazda, J. Harris, M. Curtis, G. W. Hoagland, and M. W. Serafini. 2023. *Achieving behavioral health care integration in rural America.* Washington, DC. Bipartisan Policy Center.

Sylvester, C. M., M. J. Myers, M. T. Perino, S. Kaplan, J. K. Kenley, T. A. Smyser, B. B. Warner, D. M. Barch, D. S. Pine, and J. L. Luby. 2021. Neonatal brain response to deviant auditory stimuli and relation to maternal trait anxiety. *American Journal of Psychiatry* 178(8):771–778.

Tabb, K. M., D. C. Beck, A. Tilea, S. Bell, G. A. Sugg, A. Vance, A. Schroeder, L. Admon, and K. Zivin. 2023. The relationship between diagnosed antenatal depression and anxiety and adverse birth outcomes between 2009 and 2020. *General Hospital Psychiatry* 85:239–242.

Thurston, R. C., Y. Chang, D. J. Buysse, M. H. Hall, and K. A. Matthews. 2019. Hot flashes and awakenings among midlife women. *Sleep* 42(9).

Tijhuis, M., J. De Jong-Gierveld, E. Feskens, and D. Kromhout. 1999. Changes in and factors related to loneliness in older men. The Zutphen elderly study. *Age and Ageing* 28(5):491–495.

Tucker, J. R., J. H. Hammer, D. L. Vogel, R. L. Bitman, N. G. Wade, and E. J. Maier. 2013. Disentangling self-stigma: Are mental illness and help-seeking self-stigmas different? *Journal of Counseling Psychology* 60(4):520–531.

VA (U.S. Department of Veterans Affairs). n.d. *How common is PTSD in adults?* https://www.ptsd.va.gov/understand/common/common_adults.asp (accessed June 11, 2024).

van den Brink, A. C., E. M. Brouwer-Brolsma, A. A. M. Berendsen, and O. van de Rest. 2019. The Mediterranean, dietary approaches to stop hypertension (DASH), and Mediterranean-DASH Intervention for Neurodegenerative Delay (MIND) diets are associated with less cognitive decline and a lower risk of Alzheimer's disease—a review. *Advances in Nutrition* 10(6):1040–1065.

Victor, C. R., and A. Bowling. 2012. A longitudinal analysis of loneliness among older people in Great Britain. *The Journal of Psychology* 146(3):313–331.

Viguera, A. C., R. Nonacs, L. S. Cohen, L. Tondo, A. Murray, and R. J. Baldessarini. 2000. Risk of recurrence of bipolar disorder in pregnant and nonpregnant women after discontinuing lithium maintenance. *The American Journal of Psychiatry* 157(2):179–184.

Viguera, A. C., T. Whitfield, R. J. Baldessarini, D. J. Newport, Z. Stowe, A. Reminick, A. Zurick, and L. S. Cohen. 2007. Risk of recurrence in women with bipolar disorder during pregnancy: Prospective study of mood stabilizer discontinuation. *The American Journal of Psychiatry* 164(12):1817–1824; quiz 1923.

Vroegindewey, A., and B. Sabri. 2022. Using mindfulness to improve mental health outcomes of immigrant women with experiences of intimate partner violence. *International Journal of Environmental Research and Public Health* 19(19).

Walsh, K., C. A. McCormack, R. Webster, A. Pinto, S. Lee, T. Feng, H. S. Krakovsky, S. M. O'Grady, B. Tycko, and F. A. Champagne. 2019. Maternal prenatal stress phenotypes associate with fetal neurodevelopment and birth outcomes. *Proceedings of the National Academy of Sciences* 116(48):23996–24005.

Wang, P. S., P. A. Berglund, M. Olfson, and R. C. Kessler. 2004. Delays in initial treatment contact after first onset of a mental disorder. *Health Services Research* 39(2):393–415.

Weisenbach, S. L., and A. Kumar. 2014. Current understanding of the neurobiology and longitudinal course of geriatric depression. *Current Psychiatry Reports* 16(9):463.

Wenger, G. C., and V. Burholt. 2004. Changes in levels of social isolation and loneliness among older people in a rural area: A twenty-year longitudinal study. *Canadian Journal on Aging = La Revue canadienne du vieillissement* 23(2):115–127.

West, L. A., S. Cole, D. Goodkind, and W. He. 2014. *65+ in the United States: 2010.* Washington, DC: United States Census Bureau.

WHO (World Health Organization). 2022. *Guide for integration of perinatal mental health in maternal and child health services.* Geneva, Switzerland: World Health Organization.

Williams, D. R. 2018. Stress and the mental health of populations of color: Advancing our understanding of race-related stressors. *Journal of Health and Social Behavior* 59(4):466–485.

Wilson, J. D., A. R. Gerlach, H. T. Karim, H. J. Aizenstein, and C. Andreescu. 2023. Sex matters: Acute functional connectivity changes as markers of remission in late-life depression differ by sex. *Molecular Psychiatry* 28(12):5228–5236.

Wisner, K. L., D. K. Sit, M. C. McShea, D. M. Rizzo, R. A. Zoretich, C. L. Hughes, H. F. Eng, J. F. Luther, S. R. Wisniewski, M. L. Costantino, A. L. Confer, E. L. Moses-Kolko, C. S. Famy, and B. H. Hanusa. 2013. Onset timing, thoughts of self-harm, and diagnoses in postpartum women with screen-positive depression findings. *JAMA Psychiatry* 70(5):490–498.

Wolitzky-Taylor, K. B., N. Castriotta, E. J. Lenze, M. A. Stanley, and M. G. Craske. 2010. Anxiety disorders in older adults: A comprehensive review. *Depression and Anxiety* 27(2):190–211.

Zero to Three. 2022. *State of babies yearbook.* https://stateofbabies.org/wp-content/uploads/2022/04/State-of-Babies-2022-Yearbook.pdf (accessed June 12, 2024).

Appendix A

Statement of Task

The National Academies of Sciences, Engineering, and Medicine will host a two-day public workshop which will feature invited presentations and panel discussions on topics such as

- Essential health care services related to anxiety and mood disorders in women based on currently available evidence;
- Preparing for and prioritizing the provision of essential health care services related to anxiety and mood disorders in women; and
- Health disparities related to anxiety and mood disorders in women.

A workshop planning committee will develop the agenda for the workshop sessions, select and invite speakers and discussants, and moderate the discussions. A proceedings of the presentations and discussions at the workshop will be prepared by a designated rapporteur in accordance with institutional guidelines.

Appendix B

Workshop Agenda

DAY 1
APRIL 29, 2024
8:30AM—4:15 PM ET

8:30 AM   **WELCOME**

                Colleen Galambos, Ph.D., LCSW, LCSW-C, ACSW, FGSA
                Helen Bader Endowed Chair in Applied Gerontology and
                     Professor
                Helen Bader School of Social Welfare
                University of Wisconsin—Milwaukee
                Planning Committee Cochair

8:40 AM   **KEYNOTE**

                Schroeder Stribling, MSW
                CEO, President
                Mental Health America

9:00 AM   SESSION 1: PERINATAL

Moderator:
Tamara Lewis Johnson, M.P.H., M.B.A.
Program Director, Women's Mental Health Research Program
Office of Disparities Research and Workforce Diversity
National Institute of Mental Health (NIMH), NIH, HHS
Planning Committee member

Speakers:

9:05 | Crystal Clark, M.D.
Associate Professor, Department of Psychiatry
University of Toronto
Associate Head of Research, Women's College Hospital

9:20 | Catherine Monk, Ph.D.
Inaugural Diana Vagelos Professor of Women's Mental Health
Department of Obstetrics & Gynecology
Professor of Medical Psychology
Department of Psychiatry
Columbia University Vagelos College of Physicians and Surgeons
Research Scientist VI, New York State Psychiatric Institute

9:35 | Ebony Carter, M.D., M.P.H.
Division Director of Maternal Fetal Medicine
University of North Carolina School of Medicine

9:50 | AUDIENCE Q&A

10:15 AM   SESSION 2: CHILDHOOD AND ADOLESCENCE

Moderator:
Jill M. Emanuele, Ph.D.
Vice President, Clinical Training
Senior Psychologist
Child Mind Institute
Board Member and Secretary, Anxiety and Depression
    Association of America
Planning Committee member

Speakers:

Jennifer Leonardo, Ph.D.
Director, Children's Safety Network, Education Development
   Center
Planning Committee member

Mary Alvord, Ph.D.
Psychologist and Director
Alvord, Baker & Associates, LLC

Krystal M. Lewis, Ph.D.
Clinical Psychologist
Section on Development and Affective Neuroscience
National Institute of Mental Health

10:45 AM   BREAK

10:55 AM   SESSION 3: POSTADOLESCENCE

Moderator:
George M. Slavich, Ph.D.
Professor of Psychiatry and Biobehavioral Sciences Director,
   Laboratory for Stress Assessment and Research Director,
   California Stress, Trauma, & Resilience Network Director,
   Evaluation & Evidence, UCLA-UCSF ACEs Aware
Family Resilience Network Semel Institute for Neuroscience and
   Human Behavior University of California, Los Angeles
Planning Committee member

Speakers:

11:00 | Tory Eisenlohr-Moul, Ph.D.
Associate Professor of Psychiatry and Psychology
Associate Director of Translational Research in Women's
   Mental Health
Department of Psychiatry
University of Illinois—Chicago College of Medicine

11:15 | Summer Mengelkoch, Ph.D.
Postdoctoral Fellow
Laboratory for Stress Assessment and Research
Department of Psychiatry and Biobehavioral Sciences
University of California, Los Angeles

11:30 | Inger Burnett-Ziegler, Ph.D.
Associate Professor, Psychiatry and Behavioral Sciences
Feinberg School of Medicine
Northwestern University

11:45 | AUDIENCE Q&A

12:10 PM   LUNCH

1:15 PM   SESSION 4: MIDLIFE AND MENOPAUSE

Moderator:
Laura M. Rowland, Ph.D.
Director, Neuroscience of Mental Disorders and Aging Program
Geriatrics and Aging Processes Research Branch
Division of Translational Research, NIMH, NIH, HHS

Speakers:

1:20 | Stephanie Faubion, M.D., M.B.A.
Center for Women's Health
Mayo Clinic

1:35 | Rebecca Thurston, Ph.D.
Principal Investigator, SWAN Aging
Pittsburgh Foundation Chair in Women's Health and Dementia
Professor of Psychiatry, Psychology, Epidemiology, and Clinical
    and Translational Science
Director, Women's Biobehavioral Health Program
University of Pittsburgh

1:50 | Hadine Joffe, M.D., M.Sc.
Interim Chair, Department of Psychiatry, Department of
    Psychiatry
Executive Director, Mary Horrigan Connors Center for
    Women's Health and Gender Biology
Paula A. Johnson Professor of Psychiatry in the Field of
    Women's Health
Harvard Medical School

2:05 | AUDIENCE Q&A

2:30 PM   **SESSION 5: HEALTHY APPROACHES TO MENTAL
             HEALTH AND AGING**

Moderator:
Charles F. Reynolds, III, M.D.
Distinguished Professor of Psychiatry and
UPMC Endowed Professor in Geriatric Psychiatry, emeritus
    University of Pittsburgh School of Medicine

Speakers:

2:35 | Carla Perissinotto, M.D., M.H.S.
Professor of Medicine
University of California, San Francisco

2:50 | Carmen Andreescu, M.D.
Professor of Psychiatry
University of Pittsburgh School of Medicine

3:05 | Mary-Frances O'Connor, Ph.D.
Associate Professor
University of Arizona

3:20 | Helen Lavretsky, M.D., M.S.
Professor in Residence, Department of Psychiatry
University of California, Los Angeles

3:35 | AUDIENCE Q&A

4:00 PM   CLOSING REMARKS

Vivian W. Pinn, M.D., FCAP, FASCP
Former Director (Retired), Office of Research on Women's
    Health, NIH
Former Senior Scientist Emerita, Fogarty International Center,
    NIH
Planning Committee Cochair

DAY 2
April 30, 2024
9:00AM—1:00 PM ET

9:00 AM   WELCOME

Colleen Galambos, Ph.D., LCSW, LCSW-C, ACSW, FGSA
Helen Bader Endowed Chair in Applied Gerontology and
    Professor
Helen Bader School of Social Welfare
University of Wisconsin—Milwaukee
Planning Committee Cochair

9:10   SESSION 6: POLICY SOLUTIONS

Moderator:
Jamille Fields Allsbrook, J.D., M.P.H.
Assistant Professor
School of Law
Center for Health Law Studies, Saint Louis University
Planning Committee member

Speakers:

Joy Burkhard, M.B.A.
Founder, Executive Director
Policy Center for Maternal Mental Health
Planning Committee member

Jocelyn Frye, J.D.
President, National Partnership for Women & Families

Beth Carter, Ph.D., M.P.H.
Senior Policy Advisor
AARP Public Policy Institute

Katie Russo
Senior Director of Strategic Business Development and
    Operations
Anxiety and Depression Association of America

10:00 | AUDIENCE Q&A

10:15   LESSONS LEARNED FROM THE COMMUNITY

10:15 | Alex Sheldon, M.A.
Executive Director
GLMA: Health Professionals Advancing LGBTQ+ Equality

10:30 | Kimberly Aguillard, Ph.D.
Health Equity Researcher
Mathematica

10:45 | Nicolle L. Arthun, B.S.N., RN, M.S.N., CNM
Founder, Changing Woman Initiative
CEO of Transcending Strategies LLC

11:00 | AUDIENCE Q&A

11:15   BREAK

11:30   SESSION 7: IMPROVING THE PROVISION OF CARE

Moderator:
Nima Sheth, M.D., M.P.H.
Associate Administrator for Women's Services
Chair, Advisory Committee for Women's Services
Senior Medical Advisor, SAMHSA

Speakers:

11:40 | Heidi Nelson, M.D., M.P.H., MACP, FRCP
Professor, Health Systems Science
Kaiser Permanente Bernard J. Tyson School of Medicine
Planning Committee member

11:55 | Kirsten Beronio, J.D.
Senior Policy Advisor on Mental Health and Substance Use
    Disorder Issues
Center for Medicaid and CHIP Services
Forum member

12:10 | Ayo Gathing, M.D.
Regional Vice President
Chief Medical Officer
Humana, Inc.

12:30 | AUDIENCE Q&A

12:45   **CLOSING REMARKS**

Vivian W. Pinn, M.D., FCAP, FASCP
Former Director (Retired), Office of Research on Women's
    Health, NIH
Former Senior Scientist Emerita, Fogarty International Center,
    NIH
Planning Committee Cochair

1:00   **ADJOURN**

Appendix C

Readings and Resources[1]

Perinatal

Burkhard, J. 2024. *Comment Letter to the Maternal Mental Health Task Force.* https://www.2020mom.org/blog/2024/2/9-comment-letter-to-the-mmh-task-force.

Carter, E. B. 2021. *A Paradigm Shift to Address Racial Inequities in Perinatal Healthcare.* https://acrobat.adobe.com/id/urn:aaid:sc:VA6C2:84cb6d7f-8277–4737–9c27–817902614e91.

Kaiser Permanente Institute for Health Policy. 2024. *Improving Maternal Health Outcomes and Advancing Health Equity.* https://www.kpihp.org/wp-content/uploads/2024/04/0642_IHP–maternal-health_032524_ADA.pdf.

Lenze, S. N., et al. 2024. Elevating voices, addressing depression, toxic stress, and equity through group prenatal care: A pilot study. https://www.ncbi.nlm.nih.gov/pmc/articles/PMC10823176.

Marill, M. C. 2022. *Patients Lift Their Voices to Advance Maternal Health.* https://www.healthaffairs.org/doi/10.1377/hlthaff.2022.00798.

NPR. 2024. *There's a New Prescription Pill for Postpartum Depression. How Will Coverage Work?* https://www.npr.org/sections/health-shots/2024/03/12/1237702759/theres-a-new-prescription-pill-for-postpartum-depression-how-will-coverage-work.

Wisner, K. L., et al. 2024. *Prioritizing Maternal Mental Health in Addressing Morbidity and Mortality.* https://jamanetwork.com/journals/jamapsychiatry/article-abstract/2814936.

Zivin, K., et al. 2024. *Perinatal Mood and Anxiety Disorders Rose Among Privately Insured People, 2008–2020.* Washington, DC: Health Affairs. https://www.healthaffairs.org/doi/10.1377/hlthaff.2023.01437.

---

[1] All online resources referenced in this appendix were accessed on June 20, 2024.

Childhood and Adolescence

Alvord, M. D., and A. McGrath. 2023. *The Action Mindset Workbook for Teens*. Oakland, California: New Harbinger Publications, Inc. https://www.newharbinger. com/9781648480461/the-action-mindset-workbook-for-teens.

APA (American Psychological Association). 2008. *Society of Clinical Child and Adolescent Psychology*. https://www.apa.org/about/division/div53.

APA. 2023. *Health Advisory on Social Media Use in Adolescence*. https://www.apa.org/topics/ social-media-internet/health-advisory-adolescent-social-media-use.

Anxiety & Depression Association of America. https://adaa.org.

Chansky, T. E. 2004. *Freeing Your Child from Anxiety: Practical Strategies to Overcome Fears, Worries, and Phobias and Be Prepared for Life—from Toddlers to Teens*. Harmony Books. https://www.amazon.com/Freeing-Anxiety-Revised-Updated-Life/dp/0804139806.

Child Mind Institute. https://childmind.org.

Children's Safety Network at Education Development Center. 2021. *Culturally Relevant Approaches to Preventing Suicide Among American Indian and Alaska Native Youth*. https://www.childrenssafetynetwork.org/events/culturally-relevant-approaches-preventing-suicide-among-american-indian-alaska-native-youth.

Children's Safety Network at Education Development Center. 2020. *Preventing Suicide and Self-Harm Among Black Youth*. https://www.childrenssafetynetwork.org/events/csn-webinar-event/preventing-suicide-self-harm-among-black-youth.

Hutt, R.L. 2019. *Feeling better: CBT workbook for teens*. Althea Press. https://www.amazon. com/Feeling-Better-Essential-Activities-Self-Esteem/dp/1641523328.

The Jed Foundation. https://jedfoundation.org.

Kessler, R. C., et al. 2005. Prevalence, severity, and comorbidity of 12-month DSM-IV disorders in the National Comorbidity Survey Replication. https://pubmed.ncbi.nlm. nih.gov/15939839.

Kieling, C., et al. 2024. Worldwide prevalence and disability from mental disorders across childhood and adolescence: Evidence from the Global Burden of Disease Study. https:// jamanetwork.com/journals/jamapsychiatry/article-abstract/2814639.

Lebowitz, E. R. 2021. *Breaking Free of Child Anxiety and OCD*. Oxford University Press. https://www.amazon.com/Breaking-Free-Child-Anxiety-Scientifically/ dp/0190883529.

Merikangas, K. R., et al. 2010. Lifetime prevalence of mental disorders in U.S. adolescents: Results from the National Comorbidity Survey Replication—Adolescent Supplement (NCS-A). https://pubmed.ncbi.nlm.nih.gov/20855043.

SAMHSA (Substance Abuse and Mental Health Services Administration). 2023. *SAFE-T Pocket Card: Suicide Assessment for Five-Step Evaluation and Triage (SAFE-T) for Clinicians*. https://www.samhsa.gov/resource/dbhis/safe-t-pocket-card-suicide-assessment-five-step-evaluation-triage-safe-t-clinicians.

SAMHSA. 2024. *QPR (Question, Persuade, Refer) Suicide Preventing Training*. https://www. samhsa.gov/resource/dbhis/qpr-question-persuade-refer-suicide-prevention-training

Schab, L. M. 2021. *The Anxiety Workbook for Teens* (2nd ed.). Oakland, California: New Harbinger Publications, Inc. https://www.newharbinger.com/9781684038633/the-anxiety-workbook-for-teens.

Postadolescence

ACOG (American College of Obstetricians and Gynecologists). 2023. *Management of Premenstrual Disorders.* https://www.acog.org/clinical/clinical-guidance/clinical-practice-guideline/articles/2023/12/management-of-premenstrual-disorders.

Burnett-Zeigler, I. 2019. Acceptability of a mindfulness intervention for depressive symptoms among African American women in a community health center: A qualitative study. https://pubmed.ncbi.nlm.nih.gov/31331559.

Caron, C. 2021. *What's Going on With Our Black Girls? Experts Warn of Rising Suicide Rates.* https://www.nytimes.com/2021/09/10/well/mind/suicide-rates-black-girls.html.

Eisenlohr-Moul, T., et al. 2017. Toward the reliable diagnosis of DSM-5 premenstrual dysphoric disorder: The Carolina Premenstrual Assessment Scoring System (C-PASS). https://pubmed.ncbi.nlm.nih.gov/27523500.

Eisenlohr-Moul, T., et al. 2022. Prevalence of lifetime self-injurious thoughts and behaviors in a global sample of 599 patients reporting prospectively confirmed diagnosis with premenstrual dysphoric disorder. https://pubmed.ncbi.nlm.nih.gov/35303811.

Epperson, C. E., et al. 2012. Premenstrual dysphoric disorder: Evidence for a new category for DSM-5. https://pubmed.ncbi.nlm.nih.gov/22764360.

Ferguson, J. M. 2001. SSRI antidepressant medications: Adverse effects and tolerability. https://pubmed.ncbi.nlm.nih.gov/15014625.

Frey, B. N., et al. 2022. A DSM-5-based tool to monitor concurrent mood and premenstrual symptoms: The McMaster Premenstrual and Mood Symptom Scale (MAC-PMSS). https://pubmed.ncbi.nlm.nih.gov/35354450.

Gehlert, S., et al. 2009. The prevalence of premenstrual dysphoric disorder in a randomly selected group of urban and rural women. https://pubmed.ncbi.nlm.nih.gov/18366818.

Geronimus, A. T. 1992. The weathering hypothesis and the health of African-American women and infants: Evidence and speculations. https://pubmed.ncbi.nlm.nih.gov/1467758.

Halbreich, U., et al. 2003. The prevalence, impairment, impact, and burden of premenstrual dysphoric disorder (PMS/PMDD). https://pubmed.ncbi.nlm.nih.gov/12892987.

Hantsoo, L., et al. 2022. Patient experiences of health care providers in premenstrual dysphoric disorder: Examining the role of provider specialty. https://pubmed.ncbi.nlm.nih.gov/33978482.

Hartlage, S. A., et al. 2004. Premenstrual exacerbation of depressive disorders in a community-based sample in the United States. https://pubmed.ncbi.nlm.nih.gov/15385694.

Hill, S. E., and S. Mengelkoch. 2023. Moving beyond the mean: Promising research pathways to support a precision medicine approach to hormonal contraception. https://pubmed.ncbi.nlm.nih.gov/36332783.

Hyland, T. R., et al. 1999. The impact of premenstrual symptomatology on functioning and treatment-seeking behavior: Experience from the United States, United Kingdom, and France. https://pubmed.ncbi.nlm.nih.gov/10565662.

Joyce, K. M., et al. 2021. The impact of depressed mood and coping motives on cannabis use quantity across the menstrual cycle in those with and without premenstrual dysphoric disorder. https://pubmed.ncbi.nlm.nih.gov/33651443.

Kiesner, J., et al. 2002. Affective risk associated with menstrual cycle symptom change. https://pubmed.ncbi.nlm.nih.gov/35936817.

Lacey, K. K., et al. 2015. The mental health of U.S. Black women: The roles of social context and severe intimate partner violence. https://bmjopen.bmj.com/content/5/10/e008415.

Leath, S., et al. 2022. An examination of ACEs, the internalization of the Superwoman Schema, and mental health outcomes among Black adult women. https://pubmed.ncbi.nlm.nih.gov/34622746/#:~:text=ACEs%20and%20endorsement%20of%20the,of%20strength%20indicated%20more%20stress.

Ma, S., and S. J. Song. 2023. Oral contraceptives containing drospirenone for premenstrual syndrome. https://pubmed.ncbi.nlm.nih.gov/37365881.

Marjoribanks, L., et al. 2013. Selective serotonin reuptake inhibitors for premenstrual syndrome. https://pubmed.ncbi.nlm.nih.gov/23744611.

McKnight-Eily, L. R., et al. 2009. Prevalence and correlates of current depressive symptomatology and lifetime diagnosis of depression in Black women. https://www.sciencedirect.com/science/article/abs/pii/S1049386709000516. https://www.sciencedirect.com/science/article/pii/S0889159123003331.

Mengelkoch, S., and G. M. Slavich. 2024. Sex differences in stress susceptibility as a key mechanism underlying depression risk. https://pubmed.ncbi.nlm.nih.gov/38470558.

Mengelkoch, S., et al. 2024. Hormonal contraceptive use is associated with differences in women's inflammatory and psychological reactivity to an acute social stressor.

Nolan, L. N., and L. Huges. 2022. Premenstrual exacerbation of mental health disorders: A systematic review of prospective studies. https://pubmed.ncbi.nlm.nih.gov/35867164.

Peters, J. R., et al. 2024. Dimensional Affective Sensitivity to Hormones across the Menstrual Cycle (DASH-MC): A transdiagnostic framework for ovarian steroid influences on psychopathology. https://osf.io/preprints/osf/hp7mn.

Peters, W., et al. 2017. Treatment of premenstrual breakthrough of depression with adjunctive oral contraceptive pills compared with placebo. https://pubmed.ncbi.nlm.nih.gov/28816924.

Ramchand, R., et al. 2021. Trends in suicide rates by race and ethnicity in the United States. https://jamanetwork.com/journals/jamanetworkopen/fullarticle/2780380.

Rapkin, A. J. 2019. Contraception counseling for women with premenstrual dysphoric disorder (PMDD): current perspectives. https://pubmed.ncbi.nlm.nih.gov/31572029.

Roca, C. A., et al. 2002. Effects of metergoline on symptoms in women with premenstrual dysphoric disorder. https://pubmed.ncbi.nlm.nih.gov/12411222.

Roche, D. J. O., et al. 2013. Hormonal contraceptive use diminishes salivary cortisol response to psychosocial stress and naltrexone in healthy women. https://pubmed.ncbi.nlm.nih.gov/23672966.

Ross, J. M., 2023. Predicting acute changes in suicidal ideation and planning: A longitudinal study of symptom mediators and the role of the menstrual cycle in female psychiatric outpatients with suicidality. https://ajp.psychiatryonline.org/doi/abs/10.1176/appi.ajp.20230303.

Saunders, K. E. A., and K. Hawton. 2006. Suicidal behaviour and the menstrual cycle. https://pubmed.ncbi.nlm.nih.gov/16573848.

Schiller, C. E., et al. 2016. Reproductive steroid regulation of mood and behavior. https://pubmed.ncbi.nlm.nih.gov/27347888.

Schmalenberger, K. M., et al. 2017. Predictors of premenstrual impairment among women undergoing prospective assessment for premenstrual dysphoric disorder: a cycle-level analysis. https://pubmed.ncbi.nlm.nih.gov/28193300.

Schmidt, P. J., et al. 2017. Premenstrual dysphoric disorder symptoms following ovarian suppression: Triggered by change in ovarian steroid levels but not continuous stable levels. https://pubmed.ncbi.nlm.nih.gov/28427285.

Sheftall, A. H., et al. 2022. Black youth suicide: Investigation of current trends and precipitating circumstances. https://pubmed.ncbi.nlm nih.gov/34509592.

Skovlund, C. W. 2016. Association of hormonal contraception with depression. https://pubmed.ncbi.nlm.nih.gov/27680324.

Skovlund, C. W. 2018. Association of hormonal contraception with suicide attempts and suicides. https://pubmed.ncbi.nlm.nih.gov/29145752.

Stubbs, C., et al. 2017. Do SSRIs and SNRIs reduce the frequency and/or severity of hot flashes in menopausal women. https://pubmed.ncbi.nlm.nih.gov/28649145.

Toffol, E., et al. 2012. Further evidence for lack of negative associations between hormonal contraception and mental health. https://pubmed.ncbi.nlm.nih.gov/22465115.

Wagner-Schuman, M., et al. 2023. What's stopping us? Using GnRH analogs with stable hormone addback in treatment-resistant premenstrual dysphoric disorder: Practical guidelines and risk-benefit analysis for long-term therapy. https://pubmed.ncbi.nlm.nih.gov/37341478.

Wyatt, K. M., et al. 2004. The effectiveness of GnRHa with and without "add-back" therapy in treating premenstrual syndrome: A meta analysis. https://pubmed.ncbi.nlm.nih.gov/15198787.

Midlife and Menopause

Bromberger, J. T., L. L. Schott, H. M. Kravitz, M. Sowers, N. E. Avis, E. B. Gold, J. F. Randolph, Jr., and K. A. Matthews. 2010. Longitudinal change in reproductive hormones and depressive symptoms across the menopausal transition: Results from the Study of Women's Health Across the Nation (SWAN). *Archives of General Psychiatry* 67(6):598–607. https://doi.org/10.1001/archgenpsychiatry.2010.55.

Bromberger, J. T., et al. 2011. Major depression during and after the menopausal transition: Study of Women's Health Across the Nation (SWAN). https://pubmed.ncbi.nlm.nih.gov/21306662.

Bromberger, J. T., H. M. Kravitz, Y. Chang, J. F. Randolph, Jr., N. E. Avis, E. B. Gold, and K. A. Matthews. 2013. Does risk for anxiety increase during the menopausal transition? Study of Women's Health Across the Nation. *Menopause* 20(5):488–95. https://doi.org/10.1097/GME.0b013e3182730599.

Bromberger, J. T., L. Schott, H. M. Kravitz, and H. Joffe. 2015. Risk factors for major depression during midlife among a community sample of women with and without prior major depression: Are they the same or different? *Psychological Medicine* 45(8):1653–64. https://doi.org/10.1017/S0033291714002773.

Brown, L., et al. 2024. Promoting good mental health over the menopause transition. https://www.thelancet.com/journals/lancet/article/PIIS0140-6736(23)02801-5/fulltext.

Faubion, S. S., et al. 2018. Data Registry on Experiences of Aging, Menopause, and Sexuality (DREAMS): A cohort profile. https://pubmed.ncbi.nlm.nih.gov/29169579.

Faubion, S. S. 2023. Impact of menopause symptoms on women in the workplace. https://pubmed.ncbi.nlm.nih.gov/37115119.

Freeman, E. W., et al. 2014. Risk of long-term hot flashes after natural menopause: Evidence from the Penn Ovarian Aging Study cohort. https://pubmed.ncbi.nlm.nih.gov/24473530.

Gao, C. C., et al. 2018. Association of vasomotor symptoms and sleep apnea risk in midlife women. https://pubmed.ncbi.nlm.nih.gov/29088020.

Gibson, C. J., R. C. Thurston, J. T. Bromberger, T. Kamarck, and K. A. Matthews. 2011. Negative affect and vasomotor symptoms in the Study of Women's Health Across the Nation Daily Hormone Study. *Menopause* 18(12):1270–7. https://doi.org/10.1097/gme.0b013e3182230e42.

Gold, E. B., et al. 2006. Longitudinal analysis of the association between vasomotor symptoms and race/ethnicity across the menopausal transition: Study of Women's Health Across the Nation. https://www.ncbi.nlm.nih.gov/pmc/articles/PMC1483882/.

Johnson, A., L. Roberts, and G. Elkins. 2019. Complementary and alternative medicine for menopause. *Journal of Evidence-Based Integrative Medicine* 24:2515690X19829380. https://doi.org/10.1177/2515690X19829380.

Kapoor, E., et al. 2021. Association of adverse childhood experiences with menopausal symptoms: Results from the Data Registry on Experiences of Aging, Menopause and Sexuality (DREAMS). https://pubmed.ncbi.nlm.nih.gov/33308631.

Kling, J. M., et al. 2021. Associations of sleep and female sexual function: Good sleep quality matters. https://pubmed.ncbi.nlm.nih.gov/33878089.

Kravitz, H. M., et al. 2008. Sleep disturbance during the menopausal transition in a multi-ethnic community sample of women. https://www.ncbi.nlm.nih.gov/pmc/articles/PMC2491500.

Kravitz, H. M., et al. 2017. Sleep trajectories before and after the final menstrual period in the Study of Women's Health Across the Nation (SWAN). https://pubmed.ncbi.nlm.nih.gov/28944165.

Lachman, M. E., S. Teshale, and S. Agrigoroaei. 2015. Midlife as a pivotal period in the life course: Balancing growth and decline at the crossroads of youth and old age. *International Journal of Behavioral Development* (1):20–31. https://doi.org/10.1177/0165025414533223.

Lee, D. Y., C. Andreescu, H. Aizenstein, H. Karim, A. Mizuno, A. Kolobaric, S. Yoon, Y. Kim, J. Lim, E. J. Hwang, Y. T. Ouh, H. H. Kim, S. J. Son, and R. W. Park. 2023. Impact of symptomatic menopausal transition on the occurrence of depression, anxiety, and sleep disorders: A real-world multi-site study. *European Psychiatry* 66(1):e80. https://doi.org/10.1192/j.eurpsy.2023.2439.

Lewis, J. T., L. M. Rowland, M. S. Ashraf, C. T. Clark, V. M. Dotson, A. A. Livinski, and M. Simon. 2024. Key findings from mental health research during the menopause transition for racially and ethnically minoritized women living in the United States: A scoping review. *Journal of Women's Health* 33(2):113–131. https://doi.org/10.1089/jwh.2023.0276.

Maki, P. M., et al. 2019. Guidelines for the evaluation and treatment of perimenopausal depression: Summary and recommendations. https://pubmed.ncbi.nlm.nih.gov/30182804.

Randolph, J. F., et al. 2011. Change in follicle-stimulating hormone and estradiol across the menopausal transition: Effect of age at the final menstrual period. https://pubmed.ncbi.nlm.nih.gov/21159842.

Tepper, P. G., et al. 2016. Characterizing the trajectories of vasomotor symptoms across the menopausal transition. https://pubmed.ncbi.nlm.nih.gov/27404029.

Thurston, R. C., et al. 2008. Childhood abuse or neglect is associated with increased vasomotor symptom reporting among midlife women. https://pubmed.ncbi.nlm.nih.gov/18257140.

Thurston, R. C., and Joffe, H. 2011. Vasomotor symptoms and menopause: Findings from the Study of Women's Health Across the Nation. https://pubmed.ncbi.nlm.nih.gov/21961716.

Thurston, R. C., et al. 2019. Hot flashes and awakening among midlife women. https://pubmed.ncbi.nlm.nih.gov/31152182.

Thurston, R. C., et al. 2021. Menopausal vasomotor symptoms and risk of incident cardiovascular disease events in SWAN. https://pubmed.ncbi.nlm.nih.gov/33470142.

Thurston R. C., et al. 2023. Posttraumatic stress disorder symptoms and cardiovascular and brain health in women. https://jamanetwork.com/journals/jamanetworkopen/fullarticle/2811233.

Healthy Approaches to Mental Health and Aging

Administration for Community Living—Aging and Disability Networks Behavioral Health. 2023. https://acl.gov/programs/health-wellness/behavioral-health.

Andreas, S., H. Schulz, J. Volkert, M. Dehoust, S. Sehner, A. Suling, B. Ausín, A. Canuto, M. Crawford, C. Da Ronch, L. Grassi, Y. Hershkovitz, M. Muñoz, A. Quirk, O. Rotenstein, A. B. Santos-Olmo, A. Shalev, J. Strehle, K. Weber, K. Wegscheider, H. U. Wittchen, and M. Härter. 2017. Prevalence of mental disorders in elderly people: The European MentDis_ICF65+ study. *The British Journal of Psychiatry* 210(2):125–131. https://doi.org/10.1192/bjp.bp.115.180463.

Forlani, M,. M. Morri, M. Belvederi Murri, V. Bernabei, F. Moretti, T. Attili, A. Biondini, D. De Ronchi, and A. R. Atti. 2014. Anxiety symptoms in 74+ community-dwelling elderly: Associations with physical morbidity, depression and alcohol consumption. *PLoS One* 9(2):e89859. https://doi.org/10.1371/journal.pone.0089859.

Golden, J., R. M. Conroy, I. Bruce, A. Denihan, E. Greene, M. Kirby, and B.A. Lawlor. 2022. The spectrum of worry in the community-dwelling elderly. *Aging and Mental Health* (8):985–94. https://doi.org/10.1080/13607863.2011.583621.

Karim, H. T., M. Ly, G. Yu, R. Krafty, D. L. Tudorascu, H. J. Aizenstein, C., and Andreescu. 2021. Aging faster: Worry and rumination in late life are associated with greater brain age. *Neurobiology of Aging* 101:13–21. https://doi.org/10.1016/j.neurobiolaging.2021.01.009.

Kertz, S. J., J. S. Bigda-Peyton, D. H. Rosmarin, and T. Björgvinsson. 2012. The importance of worry across diagnostic presentations: prevalence, severity and associated symptoms in a partial hospital setting. *Journal of Anxiety Disorders* 26(1):126–33. https://doi.org/10.1016/j.janxdis.2011.10.005.

National Center for Equitable Care for Elders. https://ece.hsdm.harvard.edu.

National Council on Aging. *Behavioral Health for Older Adults.* https://www.ncoa.org/older-adults/health/behavioral-health.

Policy Solutions

Carter, B. 2023. *New Task Force Guidelines Recommend Anxiety Screening for Adults Under 65, But Research on 65+ Population Still Lags.* https://blog.aarp.org/thinking-policy/new-task-force-guidelines-recommend-anxiety-screening-for-adults-but-research-on-65-population-still-lags.

Center for Medicaid and CHIP Services Action Plan. 2023. https://www.medicaid.gov/medicaid/benefits/downloads/cmcs-mntl-helth-substnce-disrdr-actn-plan.pdf.

Diep, K., B. Frederiksen, M. Long, U. Ranji, and A. Salganicoff. 2022. *Access and Coverage for Mental Health Care: Findings from the 2022 KFF Women's Health Survey.*

Health Resources & Services Administration Agenda Overview. 2023. https://www.hrsa.gov/sites/default/files/hrsa/about/hrsa-agency-overview.pdf.

Improving the Provision of Care

Gregory, K. D., et al. 2020. Screening for anxiety in adolescent and adult women: A recommendation from the Women's Preventative Services Initiative. https://pubmed.ncbi.nlm.nih.gov/32510990.

Nelson H. D., et al. 2020. Screening for anxiety in adolescent and adult women: A systematic review for the Women's Preventative Services Initiative. https://pubmed.ncbi.nlm.nih.gov/32510989.

Onarheim, K. H., et al. 2016. Economic benefits of investing in women's health: A systematic review. https://journals.plos.org/plosone/article?id=10.1371/journal.pone.0150120.

Women's Mental Health Over the Life Course

Eyre, H. A., L. E. Stirland, D. V. Jeste, C. F. Reynolds, M. Berk, A. Ibanez, W. D. Dawson, B. Lawlor, I. Leroi, K. Yaffe, J. R. Gatchel, J. F. Karp, P. Newhouse, J. Rosand, N. Letourneau, E. Bayen, F. Farina, L. Booi, D. P. Devanand, J. Mintzer, S. Madigan, I. Jayapurwala, S. T. C. Wong, V. Podence Falcoa, J. L. Cummings, W. Reichman, S. Lenz Lock, M. Bennett, R. Ahuja, D. C. Steffens, M. S. V. Elkind, and H. Lavretsky. 2023. Life-course brain health as a determinant of late-life mental health: American Association for Geriatric Psychiatry EXPERT Panel recommendations. *The American Journal of Geriatric Psychiatry* 31(12). https://doi.org/10.1016/j.jagp.2023.09.013.

Hantsoo, L., and C. N. Epperson. 2017. Anxiety disorders among women: A female lifespan approach. *FOCUS* 15(2):162–172.

Mass General Brigham McLean. 2022. *Understanding Mental Health Over a Woman's Lifetime.* https://www.mcleanhospital.org/essential/understanding-mental-health-over-womans-lifetime.

Women's Mental Health—General

Aguillard, K., G. Gemeinhardt, S. McCurdy, V. Schick, and R. Hughes. 2021. "Helping somebody else has helped me too": Resilience in rural women with disabilities with experiences of interpersonal violence. *Journal of Interpersonal Violence* 37. https://doi.org/10.1177/08862605211016356.

Aguillard, K., R. B. Hughes, V. R. Schick, S. A., McCurdy, and G. L. Gemeinhardt. 2022. Mental healthcare. *Violence and Victims*, 37(1), 26–43.

Chiaramonte, D., M. Ring, and A. B. Locke. 2017. Integrative women's health. *Medical Clinics of North America* 101(5):955–975. https://doi.org/10.1016/j.mcna.2017.04.010.

Dembo, R. S., M. Mitra, and M. McKee. 2018. The psychological consequences of violence against people with disabilities. *Disability and Health Journal* 11(3):390–397. https://www.sciencedirect.com/science/article/abs/pii/S1936657418300074?via%3Dihub

Dunn, D. S. 2019. Outsider privileges can lead to insider disadvantages: Some psychosocial aspects of ableism. *Journal of Social Issues* 75(3):665–682. https://doi.org/10.1111/josi.12331.

IOM (Institute of Medicine). 2001. Exploring the biological contributions to human health: Does sex matter? https://nap.nationalacademies.org/read/10028/chapter/1.

Kilpatrick, K., E. Tchouaket, I. Savard, M. C. Chouinard, N. Bouabdillah, B. Provost-Bazinet, G. Costanzo, J. Houle, G. St-Louis, M. Jabbour, and R. Atallah. 2023. Identifying indicators sensitive to primary health care nurse practitioner practice: A review of systematic reviews. *PLoS One* 18(9):e0290977. https://doi.org/10.1371/journal.pone.0290977.

Manning, R. B., III, R. Cipollina, S. R. Lowe, K. R. Bogart, J. M. Ostrove, J. M. Adler, M. R. Nario-Redmond, and K. Wang. 2023. Barriers to mental health service use among people with disabilities during the COVID-19 pandemic. *Rehabilitation Psychology* 68(4):351–361. https://doi.org/10.1037/rep0000512.

National Alliance on Mental Illness—Ohio. 2021. *Women and Mental Health.* https://namiohio.org/women-and-mental-health.

National Institute of Mental Health. n.d. *Women and Mental Health.* https://www.nimh.nih.gov/health/topics/women-and-mental-health.

Women's Anxiety Disorders

Anxiety & Depression Association of America. 2022. *Women and Anxiety.* https://adaa.org/find-help-for/women/anxiety.

Emdin, C. A., A. Odutayo, C. X. Wong, J. Tran, A. J. Hsiao, and B. H. Hunn. 2016. Meta-analysis of anxiety as a risk factor for cardiovascular disease. *American Journal of Cardiology* 118(4):511–9. https://doi.org/10.1016/j.amjcard.2016.05.041.

OASH Office on Women's Health. 2021. *Anxiety Disorders.* https://www.womenshealth.gov/mental-health/mental-health-conditions/anxiety-disorders.

Santabárbara, J., I. Lasheras, D. M. Lipnicki, J. Bueno-Notivol, M. Pérez-Moreno, R. López-Antrón, C. De la Cámara, A. Lobo, and P. Gracia-García. 2021. Prevalence of anxiety in the COVID-19 pandemic: An updated meta-analysis of community-based studies. *Progress in Neuropsychopharmacology & Biological Psychiatry* 109:110207. https://doi.org/10.1016/j.pnpbp.2020.110207.

Terlizzi, E. P., and M. A. Villarroel. 2020. *Symptoms of generalized anxiety disorders among adults: United States 2019.* NCHS Data Brief No. 378. Hyattsville MD: National Center for Health Statistics.

Wolitzky-Taylor, K. B., N. Castriotta, E. J. Lenze, M. A. Stanley, and M. G. Craske. 20101. Anxiety disorders in older adults: A comprehensive review. *Depression and Anxiety.* 27(2):190–211. https://doi.org/10.1002/da.20653.

Depression in Women

Andreescu, C., E. J. Lenze, M. A. Dew, A. E. Begley, B. H. Mulsant, A. Y. Dombrovski, B. G. Pollock, J. Stack, M. D. Miller, and C. F. Reynolds. 2007. Effect of comorbid anxiety on treatment response and relapse risk in late-life depression: controlled study. *The British Journal of Psychiatry* 190:344–9. https://doi.org/10.1192/bjp.bp.106.027169.

Andreescu, C., O. Ajilore, H. J. Aizenstein, K. Albert, M. A. Butters, B. A. Landman, H. T. Karim, R. Krafty, and W. D. Taylor. 2019. Disruption of neural homeostasis as a model of relapse and recurrence in late-life depression. *American Journal of Geriatric Psychiatry* 27(12):1316–1330. https://doi.org/10.1016/j.jagp.2019.07.016.

Donovan, N. J., J. J. Locascio, G. A. Marshall, J. Gatche, B. J. Hanseeuw, D. M. Rentz, K. A. Johnson, and R. A. Sperling. 2018. Harvard Aging Brain Study. Longitudinal association of amyloid beta and anxious-depressive symptoms in cognitively normal older adults. *The American Journal of Psychiatry* 175(6):530–537. https://doi.org/10.1176/appi.ajp.2017.17040442.

MHA (Mental Health America). n.d. *Depression in Women.* https://mhanational.org/depression-women

Szymkowicz, S. M., A. R. Gerlach, D. Homiack, and W. D. Taylor. 2023. Biological factors influencing depression in later life: Role of aging processes and treatment implications. *Translational Psychiatry* 13(1):160. https://doi.org/10.1038/s41398-023-02464-9.

Taylor, W. D. 204. Clinical practice. Depression in the elderly. *New England Journal of Medicine* 371(13):1228–36. https://doi.org/10.1056/NEJMcp1402180.

Weisenbach, S. L., and A. Kumar. 2014. Current understanding of the neurobiology and longitudinal course of geriatric depression. *Current Psychiatry Reports* 16(9):463. https://doi.org/10.1007/s11920-014-0463-y.

Women and Substance Use Disorders

SAMHSA (Substance Abuse and Mental Health Services Administration). 2021. *Addressing the Specific Needs of Women for Treatment of Substance Use Disorders.* https://store.samhsa.gov/sites/default/files/pep20-06-04-002.pdf.